FOOD, **FAMILY** & FUN

A GLIMPSE INTO OUR FAMILY'S
TABLE, TRADITIONS & TRAVELS

by Ruth Palau Silvoso

FOOD, FAMILY & FUN by Ruth Palau Silvoso

TRANSFORM OUR WORLD
P.O. Box 20310
San Jose, CA 95160-0310

ISBN: 978-1-5323-1825-2

Cover & Book Design by www.i6graphics.com

Printed in Santa Clara, CA, USA
First Edition

Contact for bulk and wholesale purchase: info@transformourworld.org

www.transformourworld.org

TABLE OF CONTENTS

Welcome to our Home!

This book is the result of questions people usually ask, such as: What dishes do you like best? What do you do around the house as a family? How do you balance family and ministry, or family and work?

Since family is so important to all of us, I organized my answers under four themes: prayer, ministry, food and fun. Why? Because of what they have in common: the family that eats, has fun, prays and ministers together *stays together*! We have to eat every day, so it is wise to put enthusiasm and thought into cooking and eating since God gives us everything to enjoy. It is also the time of the day when we get everybody around the same table, giving us an opportunity to catch up, pray, have fun and talk.

We have wonderful memories of conversations, laughter and fun at dinnertime. When our daughters were growing up, we made it a point to always eat together. Our girls were welcome to bring friends over, too. Birthdays were special celebrations, making it a memorable day for everyone, and more so for the birthday person.

Now that they are married and have families of their own, we celebrate every holiday together with traditions held dear by our children and grandchildren, including some special dishes. I am always blessed when our granddaughters ask me, "Lela, may we have the recipe?" (Lela is what the grandchildren call me!)

As a wife and mother, together with my husband Ed, I always wanted to instill in our children and grandchildren the importance of a united family since the opposite causes fear, anxiety and uncertainty about the future, especially in the children. A strong family provides a pool of love, commitment and honesty to grow up true to godly values so we can serve God and others.

The environment and rituals of the kitchen and dining room are where the family comes together *naturally*. It is always a joy to think that after a hard day's work we can all have a good time around the table. That is when traditions are built that help us understand who we are and where we come from, and define us as a family.

In this book you will find typical Argentine specialties, as well as some Italian dishes that we enjoy eating since it is part of our heritage on Ed's side. We also take pleasure in French cuisine from my side of the family, and of course you will see some classic American dishes, too. These are recipes for simple everyday meals that anyone can prepare, whether you prefer ready to serve food or to make it from scratch. This is not a diet book but a collection of some of our favorite recipes and memorable stories and photos from meals and ministry trips, plus some key principles to strengthen the family.

May God's blessing be poured upon you and your loved ones as you cook, pray, have fun and eat!

~ Ruth Palau Silvoso

Love Part 1: From Ed to Ruth

a rose every day...

Love is what holds a family together, and demonstrating love is important for a couple, but also for the children and grandchildren. When we show love to each other in tangible ways (flowers, poems, etc.) that they witness, it plants seeds that help them envision a loving future.

Ed is a romantic. We usually travel together, but when he has to go by himself, he leaves me notes and sends me flowers. My favorite memory is of a long trip when he sent a rose for each day we were apart, along with the lyrics to a song that in Spanish goes like this:

You will receive a rose
every day that we are apart
To comfort you
when nostalgia becomes too hard
You are the owner
of all my tender feelings
I wish I was able
To turn those roses into stars
and deposit them quietly
on your pillow
To illuminate your dreams
every night...

When we celebrated our 25th wedding anniversary, Ed wrote and read this at the altar:

> When I first saw you,
> it was like gazing straight into the sun.
> So much light flooded my soul
> that I have not been able to look at anyone else.
> Every time I look into your eyes,
> I find myself sailing an endless sea of emeralds.
> A sea so immense that after 25 years
> I have yet to see shore for the first time.
> A sea so deep that its biggest storm cannot create
> waves big enough to unsettle its depth.
>
> Without you I am a ship with no port,
> A night with no stars, a creek with no pebbles,
> A beach with no sand, a river with no shores,
> An ocean with no tides, a rainbow with no colors.
> When I hear your voice, music floods my soul.
> Your words explode into a symphony
> So sweet, so melodious, so intriguing,
> so challenging.
>
> Without you I am lost,
> As impossible as a song without words.
> You are so much a part of who I am
> that without you I am no longer me.
> I simply cease to be.
>
> With you, by God's grace, I am everything God
> designed me to be. Ruthie, I love you! I always will!

Every morning we have breakfast and devotions together before anything else. We take turns bringing it to the bedroom where we read the Bible, listen to worship music, and pray. These times are the anchor for everything else we do for the rest of the day. Love is like a beautiful flower...it is meant to be seen.

Jesica's Tribute

I am so excited that my precious mom has finally put our family's favorite recipes into a book, along with some special memories. When I reflect on the loving and nurturing role my mom has played in my life, her delicious meals are a big part of my fondest recollections.

Some of my earliest memories are of my mom in the kitchen preparing food for my family with so much dedication and joy.

When I was a little girl, we moved from Argentina to the United States and we were all homesick. My mom helped us make the transition to our new home by continuing to prepare our favorite Argentine meals. Now, this was not an easy feat! In the '80s there were no "instant" Argentine food options available. Everything had to be made from scratch, and that's just what she did. My mom would make homemade pizzas, pastas, milanesas and empanadas every week.

My school friends would often ask me what my mom was doing when she was making the "tapas" (homemade dough) for the empanadas. They had never seen anyone make "tapas" before, and they had no idea what an empanada even was. However, once they had tasted her empanadas, they would always ask to come over on the nights we were eating them.

When the neighborhood kids would be eating ice cream and brownies for dessert, my mom would have spent hours making the dough for Argentine "pastelitos" (a labor intensive pastry) for our dessert. In

school, when my friends were having Peanut Butter and Jelly sandwiches for lunch, my mom had packed me a "milanesa" sandwich on a French baguette, complete with lettuce and tomatoes. I was always thankful and excited to have her food with me at school. It was truly a comfort and a treat.

On the weekends, my parents would make meal times extra festive and fun by preparing the most delicious "Argentine Asados" (BBQ). They would grill short ribs, juicy steaks, and top the meat off with chimichurri. For the after dinner entertainment, my dad would prepare slideshows to traditional Argentine music.

Yes, as archaic as that sounds, slideshows were the equivalent to streaming a Netflix movie today. The slideshows eased our homesickness with pictures of our Argentine family, home, and animals we were missing. My dad would also serve us cappuccinos after dinner. A good strong cup of coffee is another Argentine staple that we all enjoyed together.

Looking back, I truly appreciate how my parents prioritized dinnertime.

As kids, we knew that no matter how busy our schedules were, we could always count on connecting as a family over dinner.

I'm so grateful that my parents were intentional to protect the table atmosphere to ensure it was a safe place we could look forward to. They lovingly enforced a "no criticizing zone" to keep it delightful and life-giving.

My mom and dad also utilized dinnertime to share uplifting stories and testimonies of what the Lord was doing all over the world. When we had pastors and missionaries over for a meal, my parents would ask them to share what they were seeing the Lord do and it was always so exciting to hear. Those stories built our faith tremendously.

I'll never forget how after the devastating 1989 Loma Prieta earthquake, we were one of the few families on the block that had a home cooked dinner. My mom had started dinner earlier than usual and her chicken and vegetable dish had just come out of the oven moments before the ground began to shake. Though we were without power that night, we had a delicious meal, complete with my mom's lemon meringue pie for dessert. It was so comforting to have her food after such a terrifying day.

Cooking is one of my mom's "love languages."

Even to this day, if we are not feeling well, she is the first to run over a pot of her homemade soup. We have jokingly nicknamed her chicken soup, "The Lazarus Soup," as it's so healthy it helps one come "back to life!"

My Mom helped me through my pregnancy cravings by helping make my family's meals when I was too nauseated to be around food. And after every birth and surgery, she always lovingly brought my sisters and I our favorite foods which helped aid our recoveries.

I truly praise the Lord for the fun we had growing up as a family. The joy and laughter we shared, and still do to this day at the dinner table, are treasures I will always hold dear to my heart.

I am so blessed by this book, as it allows the world a small glimpse into the heart of my mom who, along with my amazing dad, faithfully loved us unconditionally, prayed for us daily, and supplemented our bodies with delicious meals. May this book bless and inspire you to savor every moment with your family around the dinner table tonight.

~ Jesica MacNaughton

TRAVEL STORIES
ITALY: The Land With No Bad Meals

While on a ministry trip in northern Africa, we crossed the Mediterranean to visit Ed's ancestral relatives in Gorzegno, Italy. Ed's mom was born there and left with her parents when she was two-years-old. It was an incredible time! All the living relatives were waiting for us by the Catholic Church in the main square of this picturesque village high in the mountain, north of Torino. Among a host of smiling grand uncles and grand aunties with their children and grandchildren was a 98-year-old sister-in-law to Ed's grandpa. It was very Italian!

Ed's grandparents grew up nearby and both sides of the family were well represented. Emotions were in full display as they met their Argentine descendants (us) for the first time. They showed us pictures of Ed's grandparents when they lived there and gave us a tour of their ancestral homes. Our grandkids were impressed with the sight of cows sleeping under the farm house!

Following the effusive welcome, with plenty of hugs and kisses, we went to eat, of course, in a typical Italian patio dotted with cypress and olive trees.

They brought dish after dish of homemade pasta, and wine from their own vineyards and wineries.

As the dessert was being served, Ed served the spiritual food. He told them how his family found the Lord in Argentina and how God miraculously healed him of an incurable disease. All of them were touched and some were in tears. The next day they came to hear him at the church we were ministering in. They had never been to an evangelical church before, and they got to hear the gospel for the first time! It was a very memorable ministry and family time.

Italy is a country where we've never had a bad meal. Every region has its own culinary specialties. Italians take pride in their cooking, and they enjoy not only eating food but talking about it, too! Each dish is discussed in minutiae detail. In Napoli, we had so much pizza that we couldn't eat it for awhile afterwards, but it was great!

The fish we had In Venice was so good that now Ed (who is not a fish lover) eats it more often.

We sat on the Piazza San Marco savoring a real Italian cappuccino and watched the hundreds of pigeons take off and fly. In Venice, you can hear seagulls calling, gondoliers singing, vendors hawking goods, and tourists speaking a world of languages. What you won't hear are cars, buses or motorcycles since the city is built on the water.

The best thing to do in Venice is to tour the Grand Canal looking at the fabulous palazzos along its banks and to get to St. Mark's Plaza to explore this spectacular Duomo.

Then you are ready to go and eat again!

PASTA, PASTA!

The Italians can never have too much pasta, and they live long, happy lives.

I read in Sophia Loren's cookbook, *Recipes and Memories,* that any time she has some spare time and is by herself, she makes tomato sauce, freezes it, and when she is hungry she boils some pasta and has a quick and tasty meal.

She also writes that after the war, when she was trying to get started in movies, she didn't have a lot of money. So she and her mother would stay in cheap hotels and cook spaghetti and tomato sauce in the room!

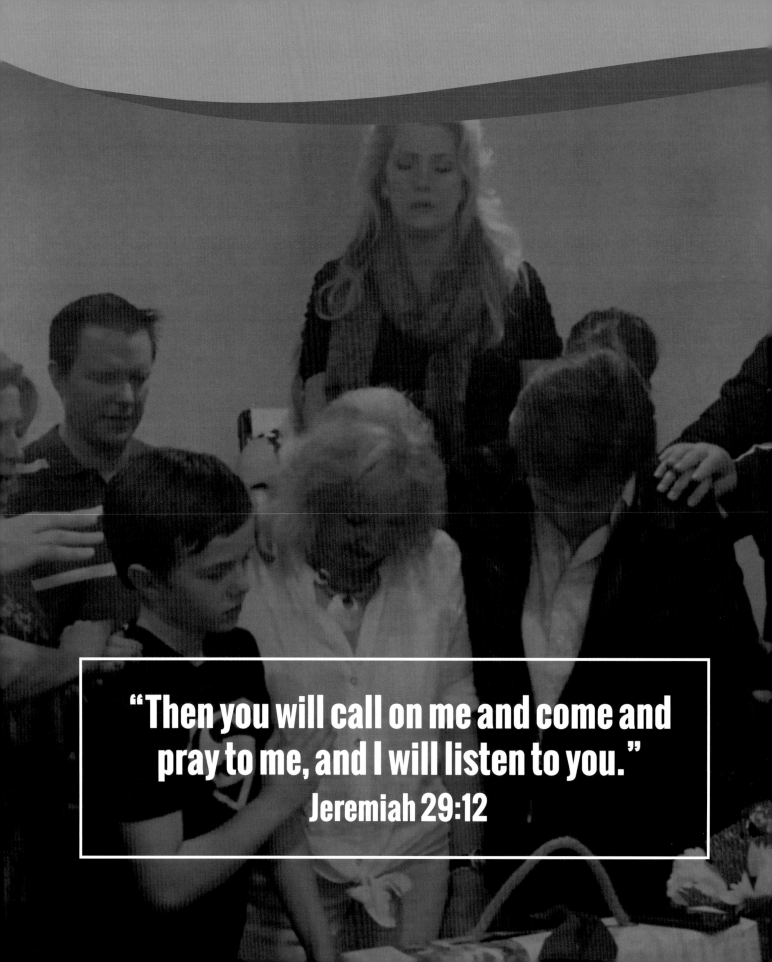

"Then you will call on me and come and pray to me, and I will listen to you."
Jeremiah 29:12

Slice of Life:
The Family that PRAYS Together
STAYS TOGETHER

I have found that, after Jesus, the main ingredient to have a happy family is prayer.

Ed and I have always been intentional about making prayer a central part of everything we did as a family, allowing it to flow naturally through the day. We would pray spontaneously with our daughters at meal times, before leaving for school, while driving in the car, and before bedtime. These were short, simple prayers inviting the Holy Spirit into whatever we were doing, turning prayer into a lifestyle and not a task.

We wrote the names of our neighbors and placed them in a glass jar. At dinnertime we would each pick a name and pray for them as part of saying grace for the food.

At bedtime, we would ask our girls for their prayer needs. I kept a journal where I wrote down their requests and recorded the answers to those prayers. It is such a faith-builder today to look back and see the power and the faithfulness of God reflected in the miracles documented in that journal.

Prayer is powerful and an essential ingredient to a happy and blessed family. Our God is faithful and He hears and answers us. Therefore, never miss an opportunity to pray with and for your loved ones. Also, ask your children to pray for you. Make it a two-way street. Nothing, absolutely nothing, brings a family closer than coming together into God's presence.

In 2005, Ed was on a very intense ministry trip in Argentina. The day he was flying home, I was with one of our daughters and granddaughters in the car. She was 4-years-old at the time. All of a sudden, she cried out, "Stop the car!" We pulled over, not knowing what was happening. She told us, "We must pray for Lelo (Ed) right now; he needs help!" We interceded for him, and I looked at my watch, knowing Ed's plane had just taken off from Argentina.

The next morning, Ed told us how at exactly that time, the plane got out of control. Ed never gets scared, but he said that he was very concerned because he could see the plane diving and the pilot alerting the passengers about the danger. Ed prayed, "Lord, alert the intercessors; we need help!" Little did he know that our little but highly sensitive intercessor was already in the Spirit thousands of miles away. That is how it works when kids are trained to pray and they are connected to the Lord.

Breakfast

Traditional English Scones

Cinnamon Rolls (or Plain Dinner Rolls)

Cheese Souffle

Morning Smoothie

Company Eggs

Canadian Granola

Makes 12 Scones

Traditional English Scones

Ingredients

2 ½ cups all purpose flour
½ cup bread flour
6 tbsp sugar
1 ½ tbsp baking powder
¾ tsp salt
4 ½ tbsp chilled unsalted butter, in pieces
1 cup whole milk
2 large eggs
1 large egg yolk
1 cup raisins or blueberries (optional)
1 egg yolk beaten with 2 tbsp water (egg wash)
Strawberry preserves or lemon curd and
Devonshire cream (our preference!)

Preparation

Pre-heat oven to 375°. Butter and flour heavy large cookie sheet. Mix first five ingredients in large bowl. Add butter and cut in until mixture resembles fine meal. Add milk, eggs and yolk, then raisins (or blueberries if desired) until thoroughly incorporated, taking care not to overwork the dough. Turn dough out onto lightly floured surface. Press dough into 1" thick rounds using 3" floured cookie cutter. Gather scraps and reform to cut additional rounds. Transfer rounds to prepared cookie sheet, spacing evenly. Brush with egg wash. Refrigerate 15 min. Bake until golden brown, about 25 min. Serve warm with preserves.

I grew up enjoying English tea time with scones and "tea sandwiches" because my grandfather was from Great Britain. Tea can be enjoyed in a variety of ways, but the ideal way to prepare it is by using loose tea leaves instead of tea bags. The water should be boiling hot, served from a silver kettle into bone china cups. Try it and you'll feel like royalty!

After our girls got married, we invited them to come over to our house to join us on Sundays for a "High Tea." It was always such a beautiful time to share together.

VALENTINE'S BREAKFAST

Ed always brings me a special breakfast for my birthday and for Valentine's Day. He writes me a romantic letter, cuts flowers from our garden, and makes his famous "Flambé French Toast" with sliced, caramelized bananas.

The term flambé is a French word meaning "flaming" or "flamed." Flambé means to ignite foods that have liquor. This is done for dramatic effect and to develop the rich flavor of the liqueur in the food without adding the alcohol. Family and friends are always impressed when you serve a flambé dish. You do have to use extreme caution, however, so I am not including the recipe here. Sorry, but it will have to remain Ed's secret recipe!

Serves: 4-6

Cinnamon Rolls (or Plain Dinner Rolls)

Ingredients

½ cup shortening
¼ cup sugar
1 tsp salt
1 cup boiling water
1 egg
1 pkg yeast
2 ¾ cup flour

Preparation

Place shortening, sugar and salt in a mixing bowl and add boiling water. When ingredients have melted and cooled, add egg and mix. Sprinkle yeast on top and let sit for 30 sec. Stir in flour (should be sticky but start to pull away from sides of the bowl). Let rise for 1 hr or until doubled. Punch down dough. Refrigerate 5 hrs or overnight.

FOR DINNER ROLLS: roll out dough and dot with butter or margarine. Fold in on self and dot again with butter (up to ½ stick). Cut and roll into crescent rolls or clover rolls. Let rise for one hour. Bake at 375-400° for 20 min or until brown.

FOR CINNAMON ROLLS: do same as above (dot twice with butter). Roll out dough for a third time into a large rectangle. Brush with melted butter and sprinkle with cinnamon, sugar and raisins (optional). Roll tightly from long side and cut slices from roll. Place on greased pan, let rise one hr and bake at 375-400° for 20 min or until brown.

½ cube butter, melted
½ cup brown sugar
¼ cup corn syrup
¼ tsp salt
Boil for 1-2 minutes, remove from heat and add 1 tsp vanilla. Pour over baked cinnamon rolls and bake another few min until bubbly.

Topping: As rolls are cooling, mix powdered sugar, 1 tsp honey, 1 tsp vanilla and enough water to make a drizzle topping.

HEALTHY ALTERNATIVE: You can substitute all-purpose white flour for whole wheat, organic or rye, and there are gluten-free flours in most stores nowadays.

Cheese Souffle

Ingredients

2 tbsp butter
2 tbsp flour
¾ cup milk
¼ lb sharp Cheddar cheese, grated
1 tsp Worcestershire sauce
Pinch of salt and cayenne pepper
2 large eggs (extra egg white recommended)

Preparation

Pre-heat oven to 350°. In saucepan, melt butter over low heat and add flour. Stir with wooden spoon until blended. Continue cooking, approx. 2 min. Heat milk in a separate pan. Add milk to butter and flour mixture all at once and stir vigorously with whisk. Continue stirring and heating to thicken mixture.

Add cheese a handful at a time, stir until melted. Season to taste with salt, Worcestershire sauce, and cayenne pepper. Remove from heat and add egg yolks one at a time. Set saucepan aside and let cool. Beat egg whites until they stand in peaks but not to dryness. Cut and fold egg whites into cheese sauce with whisk.

Pour into lightly greased casserole dish (loaf pan works for this size recipe). Bake at 350° for 30-35 min.
Note: Recipe doubles beautifully. When doubling, bake for approx. 45-50 min.

Morning Smoothie

Ingredients

1 banana
1 cup berries, fresh or frozen (strawberries, blueberries, etc.)
1 cup coconut water
1 tsp vanilla
1 tbsp hemp protein powder

Preparation

Blend all ingredients for 1 min.

EAT BREAKFAST LIKE A KING

There may be something to the old adage, "Eat breakfast like a king, lunch like a prince, and dinner like a pauper."

It is very important to start the day with a healthy breakfast, and that's something Ed and I try to do.

We like oatmeal with raisins, cinnamon, organic flaxseed and chia, and sometimes we have yogurt with berries. Twice a week we have scrambled eggs or a hardboiled egg with olive oil and a slice of toast. We usually include orange juice or a smoothie.

Serves: 10

Company Eggs

Ingredients

2 cups grated cheese

4 tbsp butter

1 cup cottage cheese

½ tsp salt

Pepper to taste

2 tbsp mustard

10 eggs, beaten

Optional: drained, diced jalapeños

Preparation

Spread cheese in greased 9x13 baking dish. Combine cottage cheese, salt, pepper, butter and mustard. Pour half of mixture over cheese. Pour beaten eggs into baking dish and add remaining cream mixture.

Optional: diced chiles can be placed on top.

Bake at 325° for 40 min. This can be prepared the night before, refrigerated and then baked before serving.

CHRISTMAS BREAKFAST

Every year, it is our tradition to have this dish for breakfast on Christmas morning with the family before we open gifts.

Makes 4 Cups

Canadian Granola

Ingredients

3 cups rolled oats

⅓ cup pecans or walnuts (flax and chia taste great, too)

1 tbsp sesame seeds

¼ tsp sea salt

⅓ tbsp ground nutmeg

½ tbsp ground cinnamon

½ cup plus 2 tbsp maple syrup (I always buy Canadian maple syrup)

3 tbsp melted butter

3 tbsp brown sugar

⅓ cup honey (local is best)

¼ cup shredded coconut

⅓ cup raisins

¼ cup dried or fresh cherries

Preparation

Pre-heat oven to 300°. Combine rolled oats and next nine ingredients in a large bowl. Spread the mixture in an even layer on a baking sheet with parchment paper. Bake until granola is slightly golden brown, about 20-25 min, stirring granola once. Let granola cool before breaking up. Add coconut, raisins and cherries and toss together.

HEALTHY ALTERNATIVE: This granola is great with milk for a healthy morning cereal. You can also stir some in your favorite yogurt.

TRAVEL STORIES
FOOD IN ENGLAND

In England, we like to eat Fish and Chips, Sticky Toffee Pudding, and Trifle since they are so typically English.

We also love having high tea with thin cucumber, tuna and egg sandwiches, scones with clotted cream, lemon curd, jams, cakes and crumpets.

I've included a scone recipe in the Breakfast section!

On one occasion, we were staying in London close to the Ritz Hotel and decided to go there for tea. To our disappointment, they told us that there was a three-month waiting list! The porter who overheard this could also see our disappointment and pulled us aside. He whispered, "I know how sad you are. It's terrible not to be able to have a good cup of tea. Let me tell you that half a block from here there is a very cozy tea room similar to ours, and much cheaper…"

He showed us the way and we had the best cup-a-tea there thanks to a kind porter.

In England, we also enjoy Yorkshire Pudding. We had the best one at Lumley Castle in Durham with our friends Ken and Lois Gott and their family. Yorkshire Pudding is made of baked egg batter and is eaten with roast beef, roasted potatoes and vegetables with gravy poured over the pudding and meat. Mouth-watering!

Once we were ministering in Portsmouth, in the south of England, with some co-workers from Argentina.

One of them was experiencing severe culture shock. He could not believe that restaurants closed so early, so he went scouting for steakhouses and food that reminded him of what he was accustomed to eating back home.

Finally, he found one and said to us, "By the time the meetings end, all the food places are closed, so I'm going to stay and make sure we get in before they close and I will hold the table while you come."

And he did! When we finished the meetings he was waiting with a table for our group of twelve. He kept saying that it wasn't good to minister all day and not have a good meal afterward. We laughingly thanked him for keeping the restaurants open every night for us.

Appetizers

Spinach Dip in French Bread Round

Chili Queso Dip

Hot Spinach Dip

Seven Layer Bean Dip

Hummus with Crudités

Focaccia Bread (and Pizza Dough)

Serves: 10

Spinach Dip in French Bread Round

Ingredients

1 Round French Loaf for Bread Bowl
1 10-oz pkg frozen chopped spinach, thawed & drained
1 1.8-oz pkg dry leek soup mix
1 ½ cup sour cream
1 cup mayonnaise (brand of your choice)
Optional: chopped green onions, water chestnuts, garlic

Preparation

Cut top off the Round French Loaf and remove bread from inside, cutting the bread into cubes. Set aside and save the exterior Round Loaf to fill with dip later. Mix all dip ingredients together and chill for 6 hrs in refrigerator. Place inside the round. Use cubed bread for dipping.

Serves: 6-8

Chili Queso Dip

Ingredients

1 8-oz pkg sharp Cheddar cheese, grated
1 8-oz pkg Pub cheese, grated
1 8-oz pkg cream cheese
1 ½ pints sour cream
1 7-oz can or jar chili salsa (mild, medium or hot…your preference)
1 4-oz can diced green chiles (jalapeño)
2 oz chopped olives
2 oz chopped pimentos
1 medium onion, minced
¼ tsp garlic powder
½ tsp chili powder
Salt and pepper

Preparation

Mix first five ingredients thoroughly, add remaining ingredients and stir gently.

Great for Super Bowl Sunday!

 HEALTHY ALTERNATIVE: You can replace frozen spinach with one bunch of fresh. Cook until wilted, drain and squeeze out liquid, then chop.

Hot Spinach Dip

Ingredients

1 tbsp chopped jalapeños
¾ cup chopped onion
2 chopped tomatoes (about 2 cups)
1 10-oz pkg frozen spinach (thawed and squeezed dry)
1 8-oz pkg cream cheese, softened
2 cups Monterey Jack cheese, grated or cut in small cubes
⅓ cup half and half
Salt and pepper to taste

Preparation

Mix all ingredients together. Pour into buttered oven proof dish and bake at 400° for 20-25 min. Serve hot.

Seven Layer Bean Dip

Ingredients

1 can refried beans
2 avocados, mashed (or prepared Guacamole for more spice)
1 medium container sour cream
1 package taco seasoning
2 lbs grated Cheddar or Monterey Jack cheese
1 large tomato, diced (or prepared salsa like Pico de Gallo for more spice)
20 black olives, sliced
Green onions, thinly sliced to garnish

Preparation

Mix sour cream and taco seasoning together. Layer all ingredients in order from first to last into a dish. Serve with tortilla or pita chips.

Hummus with Crudités

Ingredients

1 19-oz can garbanzo beans

1 clove garlic, chopped

4 tbsp lemon juice

2 tbsp olive oil

Sea salt and pepper to taste

2 tbsp tahini

2 sprigs fresh parsley

2 tsp turmeric

Optional: ½ tsp cayenne

Preparation

Pour garbanzo beans into food processor (or blender if you don't have food processor) with half of the liquid (reserve some beans for garnish). Add remaining ingredients and blend until well mixed.

If it's too thick, add a little more olive oil. Feel free to add more tahini; adjust salt and pepper if needed. Transfer the mixture to a bowl, garnish with reserved beans and serve with raw veggies or pita chips.

Focaccia Bread (and Pizza Dough)

Ingredients

5 cups flour

2 tbsp yeast

2 ½ tbsp salt

2 ½ tbsp butter

4 tbsp olive oil

2 ¼ cups lukewarm water

Preparation

Place yeast in a bowl and dissolve in lukewarm water until bubbling, about 5 min. Then add salt, butter, olive oil and finally flour. Knead for 5-10 min. Let rise for ½ hour. Flatten on cookie sheet or pizza pan, brush with olive oil and add salt and pepper. Let rise again. For pizza, add toppings and cheese. Bake at 450° for 15-20 min or until golden and cooked inside.

When letting the dough rise, I cover it with a cloth towel or plastic wrap and put it in the oven previously warmed for 1 min. Turn the heat off and leave it until it rises.

Evelyn's Tribute

I've had the privilege of ministering alongside my parents from a very young age and now working as the COO in their ministry as an adult. My husband and children enjoy participating in what we do also. There is a special generational blessing for your family, too!

In such context, allow me to share a page from my childhood that hopefully will encourage you.

Now that I am a wife and the mother of two very active children, in addition to being a full-time executive, I find comfort and strength in what I learned growing up, especially when I was sick.

Today, when my own family isn't feeling so well, I remember how my mom cared for me when I was a kid. I think almost weekly of how she would prepare meals, the spirit in which she did it, the love I felt from her as I ate them, and the emotional comfort they brought to me when I was ill.

The first thing mom would say as she brought us home from school sick was, "You're not going back to school until you are well," which would bring much needed emotional comfort. Then mom would follow with, "What do you want to eat?" At our house, the sick kid got to pick whatever meal they wanted, plus their favorite dessert.

Growing up, my mom literally made about 90% of our meals from scratch: pizza dough, cinnamon rolls, lasagna; you name it, she made it. She always added a

secret ingredient to her food…it was prayer. So many times I saw her in the kitchen praying over the food as she was preparing it. That one thing— prayer and blessing the food—made a HUGE difference.

Many times, our friends commented that something about our meal times felt different than those at their own house.

I think it was because mom made everything from scratch, but even more importantly, because she prayed over every meal.

When I was home sick from school, I often told my mom to make whatever she wanted for dinner, but I reserved the right to make my request for dessert! I always asked for Maicena Pudding (a type of custard made from cornstarch) and Rice Pudding. Yum! It still makes me drool thinking about it.

Now, as a busy wife and working mom who plays nurse to her family too, I often think of the way and the spirit in which my mom prepared meals. I honestly don't know how she did so much, and did it so well. My meals are not made from scratch as often as hers are, nor are they as elaborate (my son loves to remind me at just about every meal that grandma's food tastes better), but one thing I hope to continue to carry on is her legacy to cover the meals with prayer and blessings. If you never make a single recipe from this book, but prefer to read through it as I often do with cookbooks and chalk it up to, "I'll cook that someday," I hope you will catch the spirit of celebrating your family through meals and remembering to pray as you prepare them.

Perhaps on certain days it's a prayer at the microwave while you "nuke" a frozen dinner, or as you bring home take-out, or when you cook one of your newly found favorites that takes just a little longer than you would like.

Remember, prayer is the best ingredient.
Don't cook without it.

Enjoy reading this book; I pray it will inspire and bless you.

~ *Evelyn Silvoso Wallace*

TRAVEL STORIES
NEW ZEALAND & CANADA

NEW ZEALAND

When in New Zealand, we enjoy eating the delicious lamb the country is known for. Once when we were in the beautiful city of Christchurch, we took a boat tour down the Avon River. The Avon River flows through the center of the city (its banks now largely forming an urban park) and was named Avon to commemorate the Scottish Avon River in the Ayrshire hills that flows into the Clyde.

While on the tour, our guide jokingly said, "Everybody, look to the right at the American Embassy..." and when we did, we saw the familiar sight of a McDonald's Restaurant!

CANADA

Dan and Norma MacNaughton, our son-in-law's wonderful and godly parents, invited us to spend time with them ministering in Canada. We had such wonderful days preaching in Calgary first, and then we went to the small farming town of Veteran where they were pastoring a church.

They took us to see a local show, The Cotton Patch Gospel, a country play about Jesus if He were living in modern times. Very funny!

They also took us to a beautiful tea room nearby, and on another day made plans for us to go to a ranch where we would barbecue and go horseback riding.

When barbecue time came, we went to the house of some friends of theirs who were not there but had left instructions for us to "make ourselves at home, the door is unlocked, let yourself in…" Very Canadian! There were several houses on the property and we thought we were in the right one. Dan was ready to start the fire but discovered that the barbecue was locked. Norma was trying to make a salad but the counter was cluttered with dirty dishes, and she looked puzzled. Despite the house being very messy, and not necessarily ready for hosting guests, we made ourselves right at home. One of the kids sat at the piano and began to play. We used the bathroom. Ed stretched out on the couch and Benjy was looking at the family photo albums.

All of a sudden we saw Dan (who went to get the key to unlock the barbecue) run in shouting, "Let's get out of here! We're in the wrong house!"

We all ran as fast as we could, laughing until we couldn't laugh any more. We finally went to the correct house, had our barbecue there, and then rode horses on the beautiful Canadian prairie. It was definitely a day to remember.

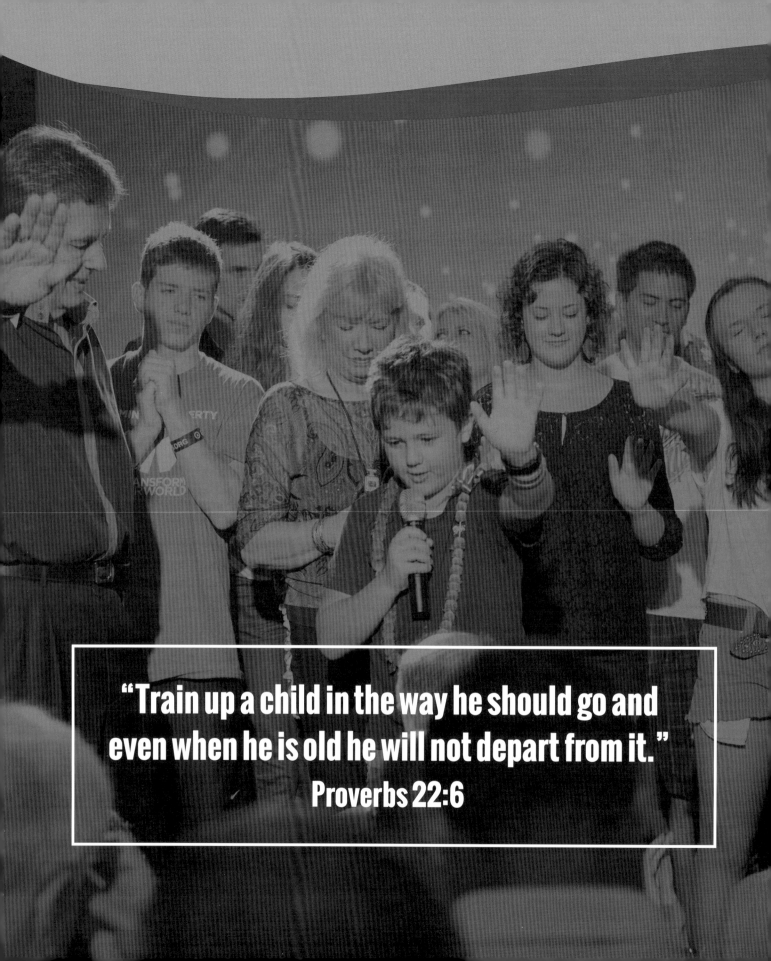

"Train up a child in the way he should go and even when he is old he will not depart from it."
Proverbs 22:6

Slice of Life:
The Family that MINISTERS Together
STAYS TOGETHER

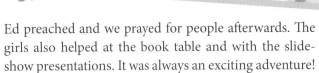

From the very beginning of our relationship, Ed and I began serving the Lord together. As teenagers, we started an evangelistic team in our native Argentina. Our team would set up on a street corner. I would play the accordion to draw attention, and Ed would preach the gospel.

Serving God as a young couple led very naturally to ministering together as a family when God blessed us with four daughters.

In fact, the six of us are the founding members of our ministry, which was literally started around our kitchen table in 1980.

In the early days of Harvest Evangelism, Ed would write the ministry newsletter and our daughters would photocopy it and set up the assembly line. They took turns folding the letters, stuffing the envelopes and adding postage and labels. As a family, we laid hands on the letters and prayed a blessing over those who would receive them. Doing a simple mailing together every month gave us an opportunity to serve the Lord and strengthen our family bonds.

When Ed ministered at various churches, we would go with him as a team.

It was never what "Dad did," but what "We as a family did." We always cast the vision that ministry is something we did as a family.

Ed preached and we prayed for people afterwards. The girls also helped at the book table and with the slide-show presentations. It was always an exciting adventure!

Every year we did a mission trip together where our daughters served as translators, administrators, and team leaders. Two of them even met their husbands on one of those trips! It is such a joy to see how they now serve the Lord with their own children. "Cast your bread on the surface of the waters, for you will find it after many days" (Eccl. 11:1).

Always try to find ways to serve the Lord together as a family. Here are some suggestions: go on a mission trip, serve as a family at your local church, volunteer at a food bank, prayer walk your neighborhood.

Ministering together with your children is a powerful way to grow as a team and to train them in the ways of the Lord, because the family that ministers together stays together!

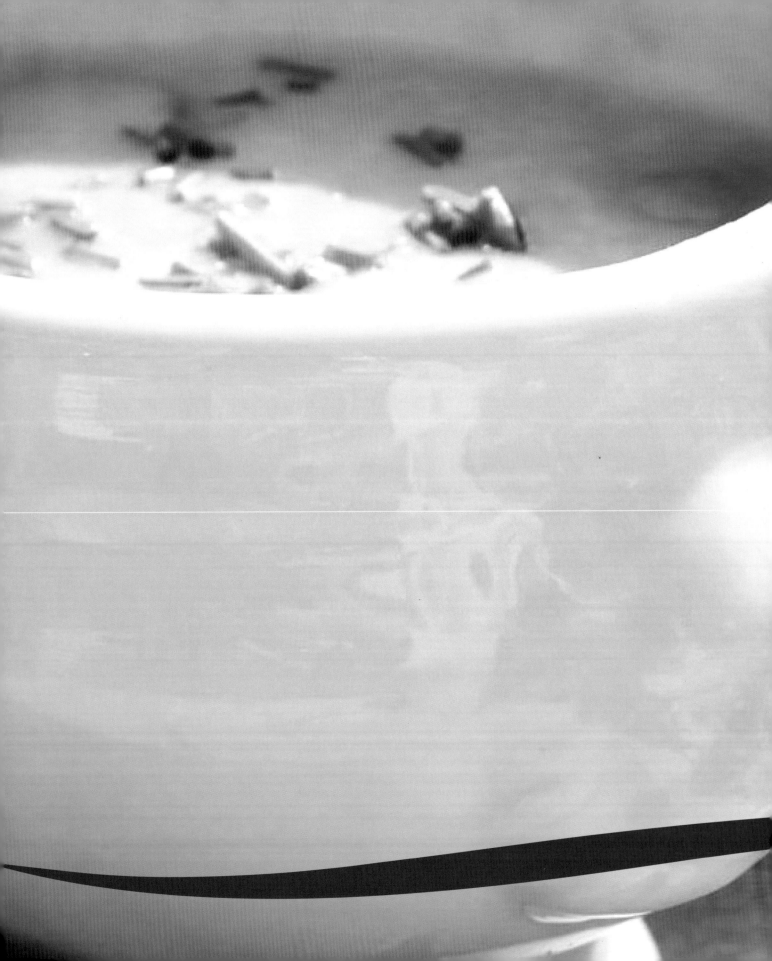

Soups & Salads

Waldorf Salad

Caesar Salad Dressing

Nice Pasta Salad

Cranberry Cream Cheese Mold

Chicken Salad

Caprese Salad with Eggplant

Mediterranean Chicken Salad

BLT Salad

Nicoise Salad

Spinach Salad

Corn Chowder

Cream of Asparagus Soup

French Onion Soup Gratinee

Leek & Potato "Comfort Soup"

Puchero

Serves: 4-6

Waldorf Salad

Ingredients

4 medium apples, cored & chopped (3 cups)
½ cup chopped celery
½ cup green grapes, halved and seeded
1 cup chopped walnuts
Leaf lettuce to line salad bowl
1 cup plain yogurt
1 tbsp sugar
½ cup whipping cream, whipped
Ground nutmeg (optional)

Preparation

Combine apples, celery, grapes and walnuts.
Place fruit into lettuce lined salad bowl. Chill.
Combine yogurt, sugar, whipped cream and
nutmeg. Before serving, fold dressing into fruit
mixture.

Caesar Salad Dressing

Ingredients

1 egg (can be omitted)
½ cup Parmesan cheese
¼ cup lemon juice (one lemon)
2 cloves garlic, chopped
1 tsp Worcestershire sauce
½ tsp salt
½ tsp pepper
½ cup olive oil
Optional: 3 anchovy filets can be added

Preparation

Blend everything together, adding ½ cup
oil slowly at the end. I like Romaine lettuce
for this salad. You can also add croutons
and avocado. One head will feed four
people as a side dish. Add more olive oil as
needed. We always sprinkle flax seeds, pine
nuts or sunflower seeds on salads to add
extra crunch and healthy fats.

HEALTHY ALTERNATIVE: We use grapeseed oil for cooking. It's 100% natural, has 0 trans fat, and is rich in antioxidants. Avocado oil is also good. For salads we use olive oil and organic raw-unfiltered apple cider vinegar with the "mother" unpasteurized and gluten free. Tahini dressing is also healthy for salads.

Serves: 3-4

Nice Pasta Salad

Ingredients

2 small onions (or shallots), chopped

½ cup red peppers

10 mushrooms

1 bunch asparagus, cut in 1" pieces

½ cup olive oil

10 - 12 oz penne or bow tie pasta

2 cups chopped tomato (fresh)

A few chopped basil leaves

12 kalamata olives

1 cup feta cheese, crumbled

For dressing:

2 tbsp chopped onion or shallot

2 tbsp lemon juice

2 tbsp olive oil

1 tsp garlic, pressed

¼ tsp Dijon mustard

Salt and pepper to taste

Preparation

Sauté onions, red peppers, mushrooms and asparagus in olive oil and set aside. Prepare pasta, drain and cool. Mix dressing ingredients and then assemble all ingredients, adding feta cheese at the end.

Cranberry Cream Cheese Mold

Ingredients

1 ½ cups boiling water

1 pkg (8-serving size) or 2 pkg (4-serving size) cranberry flavored gelatin (or any other flavor)

1 ½ cups cold water

½ tsp ground cinnamon

1 medium apple, chopped

1 cup whole berry cranberry sauce

1 pkg (8-oz) cream cheese, softened

Preparation

Stir boiling water into gelatin in large bowl for 2 min or until completely dissolved. Stir in cold water and cinnamon. Pour 2 cups of gelatin into a medium bowl. Refrigerate for 1 ½ hrs or until thickened (spoon drawn through leaves a definite impression).

Reserve remaining 1 cup gelatin at room temperature. Stir apple and cranberry sauce into thickened gelatin. Spoon into 6-cup mold. Refrigerate about 30 min or until set but not firm (should stick to finger when touched). Stir reserved 1 cup gelatin gradually into cream cheese in small bowl with wire whisk until smooth. Pour over gelatin layer in mold. Refrigerate 4 hrs or until firm.

Unmold and serve.

Chicken Salad

Ingredients

4 tbsp low sodium soy sauce

2 tsp toasted sesame oil

1 lb skinless, boneless chicken breast

¼ head red cabbage, shredded

½ head cabbage, shredded

3 scallions, thinly sliced

1 8-oz can sliced water chestnuts

⅓ cup rice vinegar

1 clove garlic, minced

1 tsp minced ginger

2 tbsp oil

1 ½ tsp chili sauce

¼ cup toasted, sliced almonds

Preparation

Pre-heat oven to 350° F. Combine 1 tbsp soy sauce and ½ tsp sesame oil and brush on chicken breasts. Arrange in a baking dish and bake until juices run clear, about 15-20 min depending on size of chicken breasts (internal temperature should be 165° in thickest part).

Remove from oven, cool completely and cut into ¼ inch slices. In a large bowl, combine cabbages, scallions, water chestnuts and sliced chicken. In a separate bowl, whisk together 3 tbsp soy sauce, vinegar, garlic, ginger, oil, 1 ½ tsp sesame oil and chili sauce. Pour dressing over salad and toss to combine. Top each serving with toasted almonds.

Serves: 4

Caprese Salad with Eggplant

Ingredients

1 small eggplant (about ¾ lb)

Sea salt and pepper

Olive oil, for brushing

2 large tomatoes, sliced

12 1-oz slices fresh mozzarella

½ cup Balsamic Vinaigrette (see recipe below)

Fresh basil leaves for garnish

Preparation

Cut eggplant lengthwise and cut each half into 6 equal slices, about ¾" thick. Lay eggplant on paper towels. Sprinkle raw eggplant lightly with salt and let stand for 30-60 min to draw out any bitter liquid. Brush with a little olive oil and grill over medium fire until tender and lightly browned, 4-5 min per side. If not serving immediately, set aside.

Put a layer of the eggplant on a platter. Add a layer of tomatoes and place the mozzarella pieces on top. Drizzle the dressing over all and top with basil. I like to sprinkle a little oregano, too.

This salad is great for summer: ripe eggplant, tomatoes, and sweet basil combined with the delicate flavor of fresh mozzarella.

Grilling brings out the flavor of the eggplant like no other cooking method so we grill it while we barbecue good meat. You can also cook the eggplant on the burner or in the oven.

BALSAMIC VINAIGRETTE: (½ cup)
You can also use this dressing for salads.

2 tsp minced shallots or green onions

1 small clove garlic, finely chopped

⅓ cup extra virgin olive oil

3 tbsp balsamic vinegar

1 tsp chopped fresh basil or dill

¼ tsp sea salt

Black pepper to taste

Chop the shallots and garlic together, then mash them slightly. Combine with remaining ingredients in a bowl or blender and whisk or blend until thoroughly mixed. Shake the vinaigrette before using.

Mediterranean Chicken Salad

Ingredients

½ frying chicken or 2 lbs chicken parts

¼ cup each diced onion, carrot and celery

Water or chicken stock (page 57)

¼ lb green beans, cooked and cut bite-sized

2 ripe Roma tomatoes

4 cups mixed salad greens

2 tbsp capers

¼ lb feta cheese, crumbled

½ cup Kalamata or black olives

1 tsp dried oregano

Oregano Vinaigrette:

Juice of 1 lemon (about 2 tbsp)

⅓ cup extra virgin olive oil

2 tsp minced shallots

½ tsp dried oregano

Salt and pepper to taste

Preparation

Place the chicken in a pot with the diced vegetables and add enough water or chicken stock to cover. Bring to a boil and cook until tender. Let chicken cool in the liquid (save broth for a thin chicken stock for making risotto or soup). Halve the tomatoes lengthwise. Skin the chicken and remove meat from the bones.

Remove any fat and shred the meat with two forks. Combine the vinaigrette ingredients in a large bowl and stir. Add the greens, chicken, green beans, tomatoes, capers and toss. Serve on plates and top with crumbled cheese, olives and oregano.

Alternative: You can de-bone a rotisserie chicken instead to save time.

Serves: 2

BLT Salad

Ingredients

2 cups romaine lettuce, diced
½ cup small crunchy croutons
½ cup hardboiled egg, chopped
¼ cup smoky bacon cubes
½ cup chopped ripe tomato
1 tbsp snipped chives
3 oz Dijon Vinaigrette (see below)

Dijon Vinaigrette
1 tsp Dijon mustard
1 ½ tbsp rice vinegar or red wine vinegar
¼ cup olive oil
Salt and freshly ground pepper to taste

In a small bowl whisk together the mustard
and vinegar, then slowly whisk in the olive oil.
Season with salt and pepper.

Preparation

Blanch bacon cubes by placing in a skillet with
cold water, bring to a simmer and let simmer
for 7 min. Drain and pat dry. Place blanched
bacon in a pan and put in a very hot oven (or
heat until crispy on the stovetop in a skillet).

Bacon is done when sizzling and a little crispy
but not hard. Meanwhile, place all other ingredients except chives in a large mixing bowl,
combine and season with salt and pepper.

When bacon is ready, add to the bowl and
check for seasoning. Plate and top with vinaigrette and snipped chives.

Serve immediately.

Nicoise Salad

Ingredients

6 small potatoes, washed and quartered

1 lb fresh green beans, trimmed

3 tbsp red wine or rice vinegar

2 tsp Dijon mustard

Salt and freshly ground pepper to taste

6 tbsp good olive oil

1 head Boston lettuce, washed, dried and torn in medium to large pieces

2 large ripe tomatoes, washed and cut in 8 wedges

5 hardboiled eggs, peeled and halved

1 6-oz can albacore tuna, drained and in pieces

½ cup Nicoise olives (or your favorite ones)

I remember when we were in Nice (where this salad originated), in the south of France by the Riviera, and eating the best Nicoise ever.

We wanted to have it every day for lunch! Our daughter Marilyn brings it in Summer to accompany Ed's yummy barbecue in our backyard.

Preparation

Place potatoes in cold salted water and boil just until tender; drain. Before cooking beans, get a bowl large enough to hold the beans generously, fill with cold water, add a few ice cubes and set aside. Place beans in boiling salted water for 2-3 min until bright green but still crisp or al dente, drain and immediately pour the beans into the ice water which will stop the cooking and keep them bright green. Combine vinegar, Dijon, salt, pepper and oil. Drizzle a little oil over the beans and potatoes and gently toss to coat.

Arrange on a platter first the lettuce, then the potatoes and beans. Next arrange the tomatoes and eggs around the edges. Top with the tuna and olives. Cover with dressing and sprinkle generously with salt and pepper.

Serves: 4

Spinach Salad

Ingredients

1 tbsp olive oil

3 oz pancetta or bacon, diced

1 tbsp shallots, chopped

1 tbsp garlic, minced

2 tbsp white wine or balsamic vinegar

1 tbsp Dijon mustard

1 tbsp extra virgin olive oil

Leaves from bunch of spinach, washed & spun

½ cup fresh goat cheese, crumbled

¼ cup roasted peeled red pepper, cut into strips

¼ cup toasted pine nuts

Freshly ground pepper

4 large marinated grilled mushrooms, sliced in thirds (Wash mushrooms, grill or sautee in skillet, toss in olive oil, salt, pepper and balsamic vinegar and let marinate for a few min.)

Preparation

Cook pancetta until crisp in oil and use drippings to cook shallots and garlic. Take pan off the heat and stir in mustard and olive oil. Toss spinach and the warm dressing. Add remaining ingredients and toss lightly before serving.

Serves: 6

Corn Chowder

Ingredients

5 ears fresh sweet white corn

3 bacon slices, chopped (optional)

½ onion, diced

4 cups chicken stock (page 57)

1 ½ tsp minced fresh thyme or ½ tsp dried, crumbled

1 bay leaf

2 tbsp potato starch

2 tbsp water

2 cups whipping cream

¾ cup cooked wild rice (¼ cup raw), or white rice

Preparation

Cut corn kernels from cobs and reserve both. Cook bacon in heavy large saucepan over med. high heat until fat is rendered. Add onion and sauté in bacon fat until onion is tender, about 3 min. Add corn cobs, stock, thyme and bay leaf. Cover and simmer 20 min. Remove corn cobs. Dissolve cornstarch in 2 tbsp water and mix into soup. Add corn kernels, cream and rice. Bring to boil, stirring constantly. Reduce heat and simmer until corn is tender, about 5 min. Season with salt and pepper. This chowder can be made a day ahead and chilled. Bring to a simmer before serving. If it's too much work, you can use 2 ½ - 3 cups frozen corn kernels instead of corn on the cob, and yellow instead of white corn.

Cream of Asparagus Soup

Ingredients

1 ½ lbs asparagus
3 tbsp butter
1 medium onion, thinly sliced
2 shallots, thinly sliced
¼ cup dry vermouth
4 cups chicken stock
½ tsp salt
¼ tsp white pepper
¼ tsp ground nutmeg
1 cup heavy cream
⅓ cup all purpose flour

Preparation

Peel the asparagus if they are large, otherwise the outer layer will give the soup a bitter taste. Trim asparagus stems and cut in 1" lengths. Melt butter in large, heavy saucepan over medium heat. Cook onion in butter, stirring often for 5 min. Add vermouth and shallots and cook for 5 min. Add stock and bring to a boil. Add asparagus, cover and cook for 5-10 min until asparagus is soft. Season with salt, white pepper and nutmeg.

Allow to cool slightly. Strain soup and reserve the liquid in saucepan. Puree vegetables in blender and return puree to liquid in saucepan. In medium bowl, whisk cream gradually into flour until it dissolves. Slowly whisk some soup into flour/cream mixture until thinned. Then add to soup over moderately high heat until thick and boiling. You may want to strain once more using a medium strainer. Save six asparagus tips for garnish. Blanch the six reserved asparagus tips in boiling water for about 4 min. Drain, cut each tip in half lengthwise and arrange them on top of each serving. Delicious!

French Onion Soup Gratinee

Ingredients

3 tbsp butter

2 tbsp olive oil

3 lbs (4-5 large) onions, thinly sliced into rings

2 tbsp sugar

2 tbsp flour

3 qts beef stock (better than bouillon)

½ cup dry white vermouth

½ cup cognac or brandy

Sea or coarse salt and fresh pepper to taste

⅓ cup olive oil

1 large clove garlic

8 slices French bread, ½" thick

1 bunch scallions, minced

½ - ¾ lb Gruyere cheese, grated

Of course I have to include this soup in honor of my "grand-mère," Matilde Flecheux, who was born in Normandie, France. I'm on the left with my sister Margarita. "Grand-mère" (grandmother) & my mother are behind us.

Preparation

Heat butter and oil over medium high heat in a large saucepan. Sauté onions until soft, 5-7 min. Turn heat to low, cover and cook until translucent, 15 min. Uncover, sprinkle with sugar, raise heat and cook stirring until caramel brown (not burnt), about 25-30 min. Sprinkle onions with flour, stirring until light brown, 2-3 min. Slowly stir in 1 cup stock. Stir until smooth and thick. Add remaining stock and the alcohol. Let simmer over medium heat for at 1 ½ hrs. Season with salt and pepper. Rub bread with sliced garlic clove and brush with oil. Toast in oven. To serve soup, pour into crocks and cover with a slice of bread, a pinch of scallions and cheese. Broil until brown and bubbly. Delicious!

Serves: 6

Leek & Potato "Comfort Soup"

Ingredients

1 lb leeks

Optional: 3 oz pancetta, sliced ⅛" thick and diced
(or 6 slices of bacon, crumbled)

2 tbsp butter

½ cup chopped onion

3 medium Russet, Idaho or red potatoes (about 1
¼ lbs), peeled and cut into 1" cubes

3 cups chicken stock (see recipe or use pre-made)

1 bay leaf

½ cup cream

1 tsp sea salt

¼ tsp grated nutmeg

½ tsp white pepper

¼ cup grated Parmesan cheese

2 green onions, thinly sliced

Pinch of garlic powder

½ tsp Worcestershire sauce

4 oz medium Cheddar cheese, grated

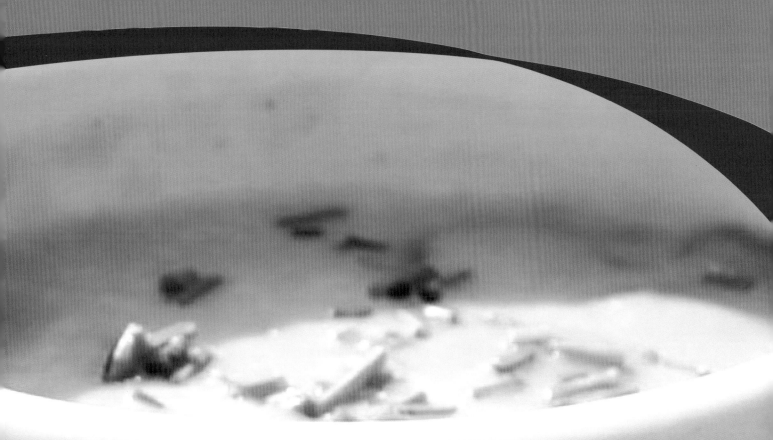

Preparation

Rinse the leeks and remove the root ends. Starting at the base, cut the halves into ¼ inch diagonal slices; stop when the tops are becoming more green than yellow. Combine the pancetta and butter in a large heavy bottomed soup pot. Cook over medium heat until the pancetta is well browned. Add the potatoes and leeks and cook, stirring frequently so the potatoes do not scorch, until the leeks are soft, about 10 min. Add the stock and bay leaf and simmer until potatoes are tender, about 45 min. Add cream, salt, nutmeg and pepper, and all remaining ingredients. Stir in cheese and serve.

How to Make Chicken Stock
(makes approx. 3 quarts)

3 lbs chicken pieces
1 large onion, peeled and chopped
1 clove garlic, whole
1 cup chopped carrot
1 cup chopped celery
1 bay leaf
1 sprig fresh thyme
Salt & pepper to taste

Rinse the chicken pieces and place them in a pot with the vegetables. Add cold water to cover (4-6 cups) and bring to a boil. Skim off the foam that rises to the surface. Reduce heat to low, add the herbs and simmer uncovered 2-3 hrs (it should taste and smell like good chicken stock at this point; if not, cook longer). Strain and refrigerate the stock until ready to use. Discard the fat from the top before using.

This is a hearty, nourishing dish very common for Argentines. Some people have a café and croissant for breakfast and put the Puchero in the pot so it will be ready for lunch. It is all boiled food based on meat and vegetables (you can use almost any vegetables you like). Definitely a comfort food and great for the winter season.

Serves: 6

Puchero

Ingredients

2 lbs soup bones with some meat (shank is good or oxtail or any meat you like for soups)

6 cups water

1 large onion

4 green onions, thinly sliced

1 leek (mostly the white part), chopped

1 turnip, chopped

1 carrot, chopped

1 potato, cut in cubes

1 tbsp chopped parsley

1 cup chopped celery

1 cup cubed squash

½ cup soup pasta or orzo noodles

Salt and pepper to taste

½ tbsp soy sauce

1 ½ tbsp better than bouillon

Preparation

Put all ingredients in a pot to boil, except for the potato, squash and noodles. Lower the heat and simmer for 2 hrs, then add the potatoes, squash and noodles until tender. Taste it and adjust seasoning accordingly.

You can chop the vegetables or put them whole and strain them before adding the noodles if you want a soup with just noodles. Some people add corn or cabbage, or even a chorizo or slice of bacon for a more robust taste.

When Ed returns home from a long trip he is usually craving Puchero so I always have it waiting for him.

HEALTHY ALTERNATIVE: We use Himalayan pink sea salt or Celtic sea salt.

Marilyn's Tribute

For every fingerprint our children leave on our windowpanes, we imprint a thousand on their souls. This is the daunting and delightful privilege that Father God entrusts to parents to impart godly identity to their little ones.

By the Grace of God, I am blessed to have parents who chose to declare my identity to be that of a person of faith, hope, and love, which the Word declares will remain.

The seeds for becoming people of faith can be planted in children during the darkest hours, as was the case with me. When I turned 7-years-old, I learned that my Dad was going to die imminently from a rare and incurable disease. Shortly after getting the doctor's news, my Dad received the diagnosis from an infinitely greater source, the Great Physician. The Lord spoke to him that he would be completely healed.

What my Dad could not have known at that moment was that the Lord was not planning on an instantaneous healing, but rather a progressive one. It would not be until I was 14-years-old that my Dad's healing would be completely realized.

As my Dad's health deteriorated, I vividly remember asking my parents who would take care of us if he died. My parents confidently assured me that those concerns were unnecessary since he was not going to die.

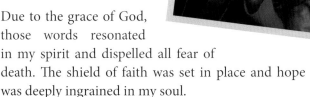

A cynic would consider that denial, but I understand now that it was faith being expressed in its proper tense, the present.

Due to the grace of God, those words resonated in my spirit and dispelled all fear of death. The shield of faith was set in place and hope was deeply ingrained in my soul.

The attributes of love are beautifully detailed for us in 1 Corinthians 13. The Word says, "Now these three remain: faith, hope, and love, but the greatest of these is love." I find it amazing that the greatest one is also seemingly the least complex of the three. It doesn't involve any lofty concepts, just simple actions flowing from the Holy Spirit: patience, kindness, protection, trust, hope, perseverance, and the like.

Let me share the following story to highlight the simplicity of communicating love to daughters.

My husband Ken and I have been abundantly blessed with three precious girls. Even within our family unit, I daily observe the simplicity and simultaneously profound effect of love. Our eldest daughter is the consummate "Daddy's girl." Once when she was little, Ken came home and I was telling him how she had spent a long time dressing up to look pretty for him. I looked up and noticed that she was listening as she headed out of the room. I saw her glance back over her shoulder to see if he would take the time to look at how pretty she was. I was relieved when, just before she reached the corner, he did in fact lovingly take the time to look back at her, causing her to break into a joyful skip out of the room.

I have seen firsthand the fruit of a parent who has invested the time to call forth his daughter's godly identity.

The results can often surprise us, as I was surprised on the day when my daughter read despair on my face and immediately told me, "Don't worry, Mommy; God will save the day!" Yes, He is indeed the world's ultimate Super Hero, but sometimes only a child perceives and articulates this truth.

In those moments, when a little one confidently declares the Truth, one comes to understand why Jesus said we must be like little children to enter His Kingdom. It is in such moments that one can rejoice in the fact that it was the Heavenly Father's fingerprints which were transferred.

~ *Marilyn Schuler*

TRAVEL STORIES
FOOD STORIES AROUND THE WORLD

CHINA

We were ministering in Beijing, China, and enjoying local delicacies, including real Peking Duck. However, after weeks of preaching in foreign countries, Ed was craving food from home. He told me, "I need food that my stomach doesn't need translation for." He wanted Kentucky Fried Chicken! We asked our taxi driver if he could take us to the nearest KFC. Our driver had a very hard time finding one, but after traversing many different streets, he finally did. He was so excited…and so were we.

One of the best afternoon teas we've ever enjoyed was in Hong Kong at the Peninsula Hotel. Barbara Chan, YK and Mimi Chan hosted us there. The Peninsula Hotel, on the edge of Victoria Harbor, opened in 1928 and is the oldest hotel in Hong Kong. Its classic beauty and timeless elegance is really something to behold. We enjoyed the fellowship with our hosts, and real English tea…in Asia!

SPAIN

The food in Spain is wonderful. The tapas, paellas, and fish dishes are all incredibly tasty! Spaniards eat dinner late. We would finish ministering around 10 PM, sit down to eat at close to 11 PM, and dinner would go on for a couple hours while the message preached was also being digested along with the food! All fun except that the next day we usually had to be up very early to preach or get going to the next town. On one of those ministry trips, our host was driving us from town to town. We usually had dinner where we preached but lunch was "on the road."

Not only was the spiritual food good, but also the delicious food he found while on the road.

We were so blessed that our host and driver had a "gift" for finding the best place to eat. Sometimes he would stop at an inviting roadside eatery, step in, look at it and get back in the car. "Not good enough," he would say. He would do that until he found an incredibly good place. Ed said he must have had a special anointing to find the best food in the towns and cities we were passing through.

RUSSIA

In 1992, we were invited to minister in Russia. I was looking forward to it because I had read the biography of a young Russian Martyr, Vania. When he was in the Army, he talked about Jesus and was punished for it, but he kept on doing it. On one occasion, the officers left him outside in subfreezing temperatures for him to die. But instead, he was dancing and singing. They said, "He has lost his mind. Bring him in. No one will listen to his God stories anymore." But when he came in, he told them, "God wrapped me in a blanket and I was warm and happy."

On another occasion, they tried to run him over with a truck, but angels shielded him. While all this was happening to him, he kept detailed records which he asked his mother to store for safekeeping before he died for Jesus. One day, she gave them to someone from America who published them in the book I was reading.

The author said that Vania had asked for prayer for his brother who was deceived by the Communist regime. So, I began to pray for his brother and all of a sudden I was interceding for Russia, and specifically for Michael Gorbachev, the last leader of the Soviet Union. But I was praying in Russian! An amazing experience! This happened in 1991, shortly before the Soviet Union was dissolved, and I heard from other intercessors who had a similar experience, interceding in Russian without having learned the language!

So, after this powerful experience, off we went to Moscow. Ed's publisher told us not to stay in a regular hotel for security reasons, but in an old home converted into a hostel with wrought iron doors. Our host was a medical doctor who became a pastor and had suffered much for his faith. We showed him how to do prayer evangelism on the streets, and with him serving as translator we led many people to the Lord. He was amazed. We then took him to a nice restaurant Ed wanted to visit (because it was Lenin's favorite) to pray there because many government officials eat there. We asked to be seated at Lenin's table and we prayed over it. Our host was so blessed and we were so happy to see him enjoy a meal at a place that had been off limits to him before.

The next day, we toured and prayer walked the Kremlin, but when lunch time came the pastor said, "I'm not eating again. I ate very well yesterday... instead, I'm going to stay outside and witness to people like I've seen you do. I haven't been brave enough to witness on the streets for years, but now the fear is gone!" Later that year, we took him and some of his friends to our conference in Argentina where they were greatly blessed.

TRAVEL STORIES CONTINUED...

NORWAY

In Norway, our favorite place to eat is at Pastor Reidar Paulsen's home. His wife, Astrid, is an intercessor and an amazing cook. She created a cake and affectionately named it, "The Ed Silvoso Cake." The first time we had this cake, Ed enjoyed it so much that every time we visit, Astrid makes us one.

ISRAEL

The first time we went to Israel was for an international conference, but the conference was cancelled by the government so we prayer walked Jerusalem and then had all week to tour and see the sights. The Lord sent a woman to us that knew about us and she offered to take us all over the region.

EGYPT

The Lord always gives us special moments while serving Him all over the world. One of those was when we were in Egypt, and the business ladies in charge of our stay took us sailing on the Nile River for a wonderful tea with luscious delicacies. Looking at the banks of the Nile River, I couldn't help but remember the story of baby Moses and how he floated in a basket down this same river. It was such a memorable time of fellowship while praying for Cairo. They were so inspired that the next day they organized a home meeting for us to teach them about transformation.

In Alexandria, Ed spoke to thousands of people in tent meetings and the Lord moved in a tremendous way.

He is risen!
Visiting the Garden Tomb in Israel.

JESUS CHRIST
DECLARED WITH POWER
TO BE THE
SON OF GOD
BY THE
RESURRECTION
FROM THE DEAD
ROMANS 1:4

"How good and pleasant it is when brethren dwell together in harmony!"

Psalm 133:1

Slice of Life:
The Family that EATS Together
STAYS TOGETHER

Dinnertime was a very important part of the day for us when our daughters were growing up.

We always tried to protect that time where the six of us would sit around the same table, fellowship, and share a meal together.

The girls and I would set the dinner table and Ed sometimes would bring freshly clipped roses from our yard to put in a vase as a centerpiece. Setting a nice table makes such a difference in creating a warm and welcoming environment.

We made sure it was a place where everyone felt loved and we could enjoy a life-giving time.

One of our favorite things was the "affirmation game." Everybody was asked to say one nice thing about everybody else. It was so edifying, and fun, too!

Ed always found jokes and riddles from the latest edition of the Reader's Digest to share at the table. Often we would laugh so hard that our sides would hurt. Sometimes he placed a tape recorder under the table and after dinner he would play back our conversations. It was so fun, and some of the things we said were so hilarious that we would play it back and laugh again and again!

In this technological age it has become extremely challenging to guard family dinnertime from distractions due to so many digital devices vying for our attention.

Our daughter Jesica and her husband Benjy came up with a practical way to combat this! It is called "The Cell Phone Box." As the dinner table is set, a designated family member gathers up the cell phones and digital devices, switches them "off," and places them in the box away from the dinner table.

This has turned out to be a brilliant way to allow dinner table conversations to flow uninterrupted. In the '80s we did something similar by placing our landline off the hook and getting rid of our television sct. Oh, how times have changed!

I encourage you to plan your family mealtimes to make them truly memorable. It is the only time of day when you have a "captive audience," because everybody wants to eat!

Entrees

Sausage Polenta

Pot Roast

Arroz Con Pollo

Italian Delight

Baked Chicken & Rice

Baked Rigatoni

Classic Chicken Divan

Argentine Empanadas

Quiche Lorraine

Crêpes with Mushrooms

Gorgonzola Cream Sauce

Milanesas

Isabella's Favorite Lasagna

Chicken Paprika

T Bone Steak

Shepherd's Pie

Grilled Salmon

Spaghetti "Al Pesto"

Vegetable "Ratatouille"

Meat Canelloni

Argentine Barbecue / Chimichurri

Sausage Polenta

Ingredients

6 tbsp butter

5 cups water

2 cups polenta

¼ cup Parmesan cheese, grated

Kosher salt to taste

Ingredients for the sauce:

1 lb Italian sausage (casings removed) or ground beef

2 tbsp cooking oil

1 onion, minced

2 cloves garlic, minced

1 28-oz can tomatoes (your choice)

½ cup parsley, chopped

1 tsp oregano

1 cup mozzarella cheese

Preparation

Brown sausage or beef in a skillet with oil, add onion and garlic and cook until tender. Add tomatoes, parsley and oregano. Let simmer for 10-15 min. Season with salt and pepper as needed. Heat water, butter and salt in a medium saucepan and bring to a boil. Add polenta in a stream, stirring constantly so that it doesn't get lumpy. Stir until smooth and cook 1 min or according to package instructions. Using a spatula, scrape the polenta into a buttered 8x13 oven-proof dish. Add Parmesan cheese on top, cover with the sauce and then mozzarella cheese. Bake in 350° oven until cheese is bubbly and beginning to golden, 15-20 min. Remove and let sit for 5 min to thicken, then serve. Delicious on a cold winter's day!

Polenta is a ground yellow cornmeal. Follow package instructions for how to cook the polenta. You can find "Golden Pheasant" brand in the supermarket. We like to buy the thick, coarse, yellow Italian polenta.

Optional: If you like a thicker sauce, add 4 tbsp tomato paste, or if you like the sauce more liquid, add 2 tbsp broth.

Serves: 4-6

Pot Roast

Ingredients

3 lbs chuck roast (choose a nicely marbled one)

2 onions, peeled and cut in half

6 carrots, washed and cut into 2-inch pieces

6 russet potatoes, peeled and quartered

2 tbsp olive oil

2-3 cups beef broth (see Puchero broth pg. 59)

6 sprigs fresh Thyme

3 sprigs fresh Rosemary

2 cloves garlic

1 cup red wine

Kosher salt

Pepper to taste

Pot roast can also be cooked in a pressure cooker and everything will be done in less than an hour! Or, you could use a slow cooker (crock pot) and let it cook all day.

Preparation

Salt and pepper meat well. Heat a large pot or Dutch oven over medium heat, then add 2-3 tbsp olive oil. Brown onions on both sides for about 1-2 min on each side. Remove onions to a plate.

Put carrots into the same hot pan and toss them until slightly browned, about one min. Remove carrots to plate. If needed, add a bit more olive oil to the pan.

Place meat in the pan and sear on high heat for about 1 min on each side or until nice and brown all over. Remove the roast to a plate. With the burner still on high, use the red wine to deglaze the pan, scraping the bottom with a whisk to get all the wonderful flavors. When the bottom of the pan is sufficiently deglazed, place roast back in pan and add enough beef stock to cover the meat halfway (about 3 cups). Add onions, carrots and garlic, as well as Rosemary and Thyme (you can substitute fresh sprigs for dry). Put the lid on, then roast in a 275° oven for 3 hrs (for 3-lb roast).

Add the potatoes for the last 40 min and check if tender before removing roast from the oven. The meat will fall apart and you can serve it with the juice over it. Delicious, especially for the winter season. The wonderful smell will fill the house!

Serves: 4

Arroz Con Pollo
(Rice with Chicken)

Ingredients

1 whole chicken, cut into 8 pieces

1 onion, chopped

2 cloves garlic, pressed

1 ½ cups of your favorite tomato sauce

4 tbsp oil

½ cup chicken broth

1 cup cooked rice (brown or white), pre-pared according to package directions

Season with salt, pepper, mustard powder, chili powder, red pepper flakes and oregano.

Preparation

Brown chicken in oil, set aside. Brown onions and garlic until tender. Add chicken, tomato sauce and broth to onion mixture and cook for 15 min. Season to taste. Cooking time varies according to size of chicken. Add cooked rice and mix everything together.

Optional:

- Add ½ cup white wine when cooking chicken.
- Add 1 tsp saffron to water when boiling rice for a nice colorful dish.
- Add ¼ cup cooked green peas.

Our daughter Evelyn loves this dish. When she was expecting our granddaughter, she would ask me to make it every week while I was praying for her. The doctor thought something was wrong with the pregnancy. Thank the Lord that the baby was born completely healthy!

This is the first dish we tried when we came to the United States in the 1970s at a home where we were staying in Palo Alto, CA. It's a very tasty and inexpensive dish that can be made ahead and frozen, and it's even better as leftovers!

Serves: 4-6

Italian Delight

Ingredients

1 tbsp olive oil

1 lb ground beef

2 cups noodles (measure dry)

1 large onion (or 2 small), chopped

2 large green bell peppers, chopped

2 cans tomato sauce (or 1 can tomato sauce and 1 can marinara)

Garlic powder to taste

Pepper to taste

Celery salt to taste

1 10-oz pkg frozen corn

1 can black olives, chopped

½ tsp chili powder

¼ tsp salt

Grated Cheddar cheese

Preparation

Crumble meat and brown in skillet with 1 tbsp olive oil. Season with salt, pepper, garlic powder, and celery salt. In another skillet, simmer chopped onions and bell peppers until tender. Boil noodles in salted water with a little salad oil. Drain. Combine meat, onions, peppers, corn, olives, chili powder, noodles and sauce in casserole dish. Cover with grated cheese. Bake at 350° for 45 min, uncovered.

Serves: 4-6

Baked Chicken & Rice

Ingredients

3 lbs chicken, cut up and seasoned well with salt and pepper (whole chicken, breasts, thighs based on preference)
1 ½ cups rice, uncooked
1 onion, chopped
1 tbsp melted butter
1 can cream of chicken soup
1 can cream of celery soup
1 can cream of mushroom soup

Preparation

Mix all ingredients well (except chicken) and place in greased 9x13 pan. Place seasoned chicken on top and bake uncovered at 275° for about 2 ½ hrs.

Very easy dish for busy moms! I got this recipe in 1980 when using canned goods was very common. I include it here for those who like the convenience of it.

Serves: 4-6

Baked Rigatoni

Ingredients

¼ pkg (6 oz) Rigatoni noodles
⅓ onion, chopped
1 clove garlic, minced
1 tbsp vegetable oil
1 small can marinara sauce
2 cups mozzarella cheese

Preparation

Heat oven to 375°. Boil rigatoni noodles for 14 min (add dash of salt). While noodles cook, sauté onion and garlic in oil. Add marinara sauce, reduce heat and simmer for 10 min. Toss sauce with rigatoni noodles. In 11x17 baking dish layer ½ rigatoni mixture and ½ cup cheese. Repeat layers.

Bake 30 min covered with foil. For last few minutes, broil uncovered until cheese is golden. Eat while hot.

HEALTHY ALTERNATIVE: There are cheese substitutes now and they have less salt.

TROUBLE IN THE PANTRY

I don't remember ever burning food, but I did have a disastrous dinner on one occasion. When our girls were 5, 7, 12 and 15, we lived on a street filled with children who played with them. One day, we decided to invite their friends for dinner, kids from elementary age to high school. We wanted to get to know them better, so I made homemade pizza. I knew my pizza always turned out right, so I didn't even taste the dough or the sauce as I was preparing them. It all looked great.

When the first teenager took a bite, he exclaimed, "Wow! This pizza is sweet like pastry!" I thought, well, that's a compliment, but another kid said, "Hmm...it is different than American pizza." My heart sank. They don't like it; how sad. Our oldest daughter came to my defense, "What is wrong with it? My mom makes the best pizza, and this is how we eat it in Argentina..."

But when we tried it... it really was terribly sweet, and pizza is not supposed to be sweet. What happened was that the night before, when Ed and I went out to our weekly neighborhood prayer meeting, our youngest daughters, Evelyn and Jesica, began to play with the flour, salt, and sugar, and before we came home they decided to put it all back in the same bag.

One of the boys said when he left, "We learned that in Argentina they eat sweet pizza." That was my worst meal ever, but I was glad that it was for the kids and not their parents.

I got this recipe from my son-in-law
Ken's mother, Sally, in 1990!

Classic Chicken Divan

Ingredients

3 boneless chicken breasts

2 bunches fresh broccoli or 2 10-oz pkg frozen

¼ cup butter

¼ cup all purpose flour

2 cups chicken broth

½ cup whipping cream

3 tbsp cooking sherry

½ tsp salt

¼ cup grated Parmesan cheese

Preparation

Place chicken breasts in baking dish, brush with olive oil or butter, salt and pepper. Cover with parchment paper. Bake for 15-20 min in a 350° oven until internal temperature is 165°. When cool enough to handle, cut chicken into thin slices.

Cook broccoli in boiling salted water; drain and place in ice water to stop cooking and keep bright green. Melt butter in medium saucepan. Add flour over low/medium heat and stir the "roux" with a whisk for about 1 min without browning until flour is cooked. Slowly whisk in chicken broth. Stir constantly until mixture thickens. Stir in whipping cream, sherry, salt and dash of pepper.

Place broccoli crosswise in 9x13 baking dish. Pour half the sauce over broccoli. Top with chicken slices. Add Parmesan cheese to remaining sauce and pour over chicken. Sprinkle with remaining Parmesan cheese. Bake at 350° for 20 min or until hot throughout, then broil just until sauce is golden.

Serves: 6-8

Argentine Empanadas

Ingredients

Dough ingredients:

6 cups white flour

2 eggs

1 cup milk

1 cup water (or substitute milk with 2 cups water)

1 tbsp salt

1 tbsp vegetable oil

Filling ingredients:

6 tbsp vegetable oil

1 large onion

2 lbs ground/minced beef

Optional: 1 cup raisins

½ cup chopped green olives

4 chopped hard boiled eggs

Salt, pepper, oregano, cumin, paprika to taste

½ cup broth as needed if filling is too dry

1 cup oil for frying

Option: Empanadas can also be brushed with olive oil and baked in the oven on a greased baking sheet at 350° until brown, about 15-20 min.

Preparation

Place flour on counter and fold in beaten eggs in center, then salt, oil, milk and water. Knead dough thoroughly. Roll dough flat with a rolling pin or pasta machine. Rolling the dough will help achieve a smooth and fairly thin dough, about ¼" thick. Lay dough flat on the counter and using round cookie cutter (or cup with wide rim) cut as many circles as possible.

Filling: in medium saucepan sauté the chopped onions with oil over medium heat. Once the onions are soft, add the meat and brown. Add raisins (optional), olives and eggs. Add salt, pepper and the rest of the seasonings. Place spoonful of meat filling onto each circle of dough. Fold the dough over to close the empanada and press edges. Heat vegetable oil in a deep frying pan. When hot, begin frying empanadas. Size of pan will determine how many can be fried at a time.

Remove empanadas from heat when golden brown. Serve hot and enjoy!

Serves: 6

Quiche Lorraine

Ingredients

4 eggs

1 lb pie dough (see pie crust recipe)

3 ½ oz smoked bacon or deli ham

2 tbsp butter

1 cup milk

1 cup heavy cream

Salt, pepper, grated nutmeg

Preparation

Prepare pie crust recipe. Chop bacon or ham into small pieces and brown with butter in a frying pan. Beat together eggs, milk, cream and flour. Add salt, pepper and a little grated nutmeg. Drain bacon or ham and place in pie dish. Pour the egg mixture over and bake on top oven rack at 375° for 25-30 min.

Optional: add 1 cup grated Gruyere cheese with the bacon, ham, or mushrooms, depending on taste. Serve hot with green salad.

I like to add asparagus or fresh sliced tomatoes on top. Use your own creativity.

Pie Crust Ingredients

1 ⅞ cups flour

¼ tsp salt

1 egg

1 stick plus 6 tbsp unsalted butter

Pie Crust Preparation

Combine flour and salt in food processor and pulse to mix, add butter and pulse until mixed. Add egg and mix until mixture begins to go to one side of the bowl.

Pat into pie pan and refrigerate for 30 min. Place a piece of parchment paper on top, with a pan on top of that, and bake at 400° for 8 min. Remove parchment paper and bake 3 min more.

Serves: 6

Crêpes with Mushrooms (Gâteau de Crêpes aux Champignons)

Ingredients

18 crêpes (see crêpes from scratch on page 118)
Salt
11 oz fresh mushrooms, or equivalent canned
2 tbsp butter
Pepper
1 cup grated Gruyère cheese
Cream Sauce (see recipe on this page)

Cream Sauce

6 tbsp butter
6 tbsp all-purpose flour
2 cups milk
2 cups heavy whipping cream
Salt, pepper and nutmeg to taste
½ cup grated Parmesan cheese
2 cloves garlic, mashed

Preparation

Prepare 18 fairly thick crêpes in the traditional way and lightly season with salt. Keep hot. Prepare the mushrooms by removing the grit, or draining if canned. Brown the mushrooms in a frying pan with half the butter. When cooked, fill each crêpe with cheese and mushrooms. Place a crêpe in an ovenproof dish, pour over a little of the cream sauce with mushrooms, then top with another crêpe, and so on. Pre-heat in the oven before serving. This dish tastes even better if the cream sauce is made with equal parts milk and cream.

You can use the crêpe batter for sweet or savory dishes.

Melt butter in a heavy saucepan over medium heat. Stir in flour until smooth and keep stirring for 1-2 min as the "roux" cooks, then gradually add milk and cream.

Bring to boil, cook and stir for 1 min or until thickened. Remove from heat; season with salt, pepper, garlic and nutmeg. Spread cream sauce over cannelloni and sprinkle with cheese. Bake uncovered at 375° for 20-30 min or until hot and bubbly.

HEALTHY ALTERNATIVE: There are several types of milk on the market that you can use instead of cow's milk. Almond and coconut are a couple of them.

Serves: 4-6

Gorgonzola Cream Sauce

Ingredients

2 tbsp shallots

2 tbsp olive oil

1 cup cream

6 oz Gorgonzola cheese (cubed)

2 tbsp grated Parmesan cheese

Fresh ground black pepper

2 fresh sage leaves

Preparation

Sauté shallots in the oil, add cream and sage leaves, and simmer until slightly reduced. Stir in cheeses. Add pepper and toss with cooked pasta. Remove sage leaves before serving if desired.

We like this over homemade gnocchi (potato dumplings) or on ravioli!

Serves: 3-4

Milanesas

Ingredients

1 lb sirloin steak (thinly sliced) or sandwich steak

4 cloves garlic, crushed

4 tbsp chopped Italian parsley

2 eggs, beaten

1 cup bread crumbs

Salt and pepper to taste

Oil for frying (enough to cover steaks, about 2 cups)

1 lemon

Preparation

In a bowl combine beaten eggs, crushed garlic and chopped parsley. Add salt and pepper. Dip steaks in egg mixture and then dredge in bread crumbs. Fry the steaks in hot oil (enough to cover them) and let drain on paper towels. Squeeze lemon over steaks before serving (optional).

I suggest mashed potatoes or French fries as a side dish with a nice mixed salad…the Argentine way!

When we have leftover milanesas, we warm them up in the oven the next day with tomato sauce and mozzarella cheese on top until the cheese is melted. Delicious! We call this Napoli style.

In Austria and Germany, the closest thing to an Argentine milanesa is the Wienerschnitzel. Once when we were in Vienna, we had the biggest Wienerschnitzel we've ever seen. It was as big as the whole plate! It was served with parsley potatoes and was very tasty.

Serves: 6-8

Isabella's Favorite Lasagna

Ingredients

8 oz lasagna noodles, cooked and drained according to package directions
1 lb lean ground beef
2 tbsp oil
1 medium onion, chopped
2 15-oz containers ricotta cheese
2 eggs, slightly beaten
2 cups spinach, washed, chopped, sautéed and drained well
2 cups mozzarella cheese, grated and divided
1 cup Parmesan cheese, grated and divided

¾ tsp salt
½ tsp dried basil
½ tsp dried oregano
⅛ tsp pepper
¼ cup fresh Italian parsley, chopped
2 cloves garlic, minced
1 small can tomato paste
1 28-oz can crushed tomatoes
1 cup water
Optional: ⅛ tsp crushed red pepper

Preparation

Pre-heat oven to 350°. Put ground beef in large skillet with oil and brown. Add onions and cook until tender. Add spices, parsley, garlic, water, tomato paste and tomatoes. Bring to a boil and reduce heat. Cover and simmer 20 min, stirring occasionally (reduce simmer to 5 min if using prepared sauce from a jar).

Meanwhile, in a medium bowl combine ricotta, eggs, spinach (chopped), 1 ½ cups mozzarella and ¾ cup Parmesan cheese. In 9x13 pan, spread 1 cup meat sauce. Place ⅓ of lasagna noodles over the sauce. Spread ½ the cheese mixture over noodles and top with meat sauce. Repeat and top with remaining noodles and meat sauce. Cover with foil and bake 40 min. Uncover, sprinkle with reserved ½ cup mozzarella and ¼ cup Parmesan cheese.

Bake 10 min more or until cheese is bubbly. Remove from oven and let stand for 15 min before serving.

Chicken Paprika

Ingredients

1 ½ lbs chicken breast, boneless & skinless

2 tbsp oil

1 tbsp butter

1 onion, sliced

1 bell pepper, sliced

2 cloves garlic, crushed

Salt and pepper

2 tbsp flour

½ cup crushed, peeled tomatoes in juice

1 cup chicken stock (can sub 1 bouillon cube in 1 cup hot water)

2 tbsp paprika

3-4 slices provolone (or your favorite) cheese

Preparation

Heat oil and butter in skillet. Sauté onion, bell pepper and garlic for 5-8 min on medium heat. Season chicken with paprika, salt and pepper and lightly flour. Drain onion and garlic, reserving oil in pan (add more oil if necessary to cook chicken). Sauté chicken for 10 min over medium heat, turning once. Remove chicken and set aside.

Add 2 tbsp flour to skillet and cook for 2 min, stirring constantly. Add chicken stock slowly and stir constantly (use whisk). Return chicken, onions and garlic to pan. Add tomatoes. Cover each chicken breast with a slice of cheese and cover. Let simmer for about 5 min until cheese melts and sauce is bubbly. Serve over rice.

For homemade chicken stock, see recipe on page 57.

T Bone Steak

Evelyn's recipe for an easy and fast way to cook a good T-Bone steak.

Ingredients

T-Bone steaks (1 per person)

Salt and pepper

1 tbsp oil

Preparation

Season steaks with salt and pepper and cook in a cast iron skillet with oil on medium high heat for 3 min on one side, and then 2 min on the other.

Put the skillet in a 450° oven for 8 min. Remove and let rest for 10 min before serving.

Shepherd's Pie

My mother used to make this when we were little!

Ingredients

1 tbsp olive oil
1 medium onion, diced
2 cloves garlic, minced
1 lb ground beef or lamb
1 ½ tbsp tomato paste
½ cup water
½ cup beef broth
1 tbsp Worcestershire sauce
Salt and pepper
¼ tsp dried thyme
¼ tsp fresh or dried rosemary
1 tbsp parsley
4 potatoes, peeled and cut
2 tbsp sour cream
¼ cup milk
2 tbsp Parmesan cheese, grated

Preparation

Sauté onion in oil until caramelized. Add garlic and cook briefly. Remove from pan. Brown beef and add onion mixture, tomato paste, Worcestershire, water and broth. Cook until everything is soft. Salt and pepper and place in a casserole or baking dish. Boil potatoes until soft, drain, and add milk and sour cream or butter. Mash well. Cover meat with mashed potatoes and sprinkle with Parmesan cheese. Bake at 375° uncovered until golden brown, about 35 min.

Some people like to add yellow corn to this dish. I suggest ½ cup corn kernels.

Serves: 3 per fillet

Grilled Salmon

Ingredients

Salmon fillets, skin removed
Olive oil
Cajun seasoning (optional)
Garlic and onion powder

Preparation

Drizzle a little olive oil on aluminum foil. Coat the salmon on both sides with oil. Season both sides with Cajun seasoning, garlic and onion powder. Fold foil around fillets and seal, leaving a few holes for steam. Grill on the rack of a pre-heated grill at medium high for 11 min. Salmon should be flaky when ready.

This is great with rice. Easy, fast, healthy and tasty! Fish is low in saturated fat and cholesterol, and high in omega-3 fatty acids.

FISH STORY
One day I went to visit our daughter Marilyn, and her first daughter who was 3-years-old at the time, was eating fish, spinach and brown rice. I was so happy to see her eating and enjoying something so healthy and with such "gusto." With no prompting, she told me, "This is very good food for me." Indeed it is!

Serves: 4

Spaghetti "Al Pesto"

Ingredients

¾ lb spaghetti
½ cup olive oil
4 cloves garlic, coarsely chopped
⅓ cup pine nuts, finely chopped
½ cup Parmesan cheese
8-10 fresh basil leaves, finely chopped
Salt and pepper to taste

Preparation

Put garlic, pine nuts, basil, cheese, salt and pepper in a bowl. Add the oil and stir. Pour over cooked pasta and toss. You can add more oil at the end, and more Parmesan cheese if needed.

Variation: Add basil, Parmesan, pine nuts, garlic and oil in food processor and pulse until well combined. Process until smooth, thick purée forms, about one min. Toss with pasta, serve.

I prefer the more coarse and crunchy preparation!

Serves: 2-4

Vegetable "Ratatouille"

When I run out of ideas for what to cook, I get:

Ingredients

1 zucchini
1 bell pepper
1 bunch of asparagus
1 onion
1 carrot
Or any other vegetable in season
that I have on hand
1 tbsp oil
Season with salt, pepper, Thyme, Oregano

Preparation

I cut vegetables in chunks or thick slices and stir fry everything in an oiled skillet or coated with oil in the oven to roast. Very easy and you can serve with rice.

Serves: 4-6

Meat Canelloni (Italian Style Filled with Ricotta & Spinach)

Ingredients

1 tbsp olive oil

1 yellow onion, diced

16 oz Italian sausage or ground beef

1 10-oz box frozen spinach (or fresh cooked spinach), chopped and well drained

1 15-oz container ricotta cheese

1 ½ cups Parmesan cheese

3 eggs

Salt, pepper and nutmeg to taste

12 crêpes (see recipe on page 118)

4 cups tomato sauce of your choice (I like to add dry oregano, basil and garlic to the sauce)

1 cup grated Monterey Jack cheese

Preparation

In a skillet, heat the olive oil over medium high heat and sauté the onions. Add sausage or ground beef and brown for about 12 min. Add the tomato sauce and set aside. In a bowl, stir together the spinach, ricotta, half the Parmesan cheese, eggs, salt, pepper and nutmeg to taste. Fill the crêpes with this mixture and roll them into tubes. Arrange tubes in a 9x13 baking dish.

Pre-heat oven to 400°. Pour the meat and tomato sauce and Jack cheese over the canelloni and sprinkle the remaining Parmesan cheese on top. Bake in the oven for 15-20 min or until hot.

This dish keeps well in the refrigerator and can be re-heated the next day. It tastes even better!

Variation: If you don't like meat and tomato sauce, cream sauce is a great alternative. See next page.

Cream Sauce

6 tbsp butter
6 tbsp all-purpose flour
2 cups milk
2 cups heavy whipping cream
Salt, pepper and nutmeg to taste
½ cup grated Parmesan cheese
2 cloves garlic, mashed

Melt butter in a heavy saucepan over medium heat. Stir in flour until smooth and keep stirring for 1-2 min as the "roux" cooks, then gradually add milk and cream.

Bring to boil, cook and stir for one min or until thickened. Remove from heat; season with salt, pepper, garlic and nutmeg. Spread cream sauce over canelloni and sprinkle with cheese. Bake uncovered at 375° for 20-30 min or until hot and bubbly.

How to Make an Argentine Barbecue

Meat Preparation

Suggested cuts: short ribs, tri-tip or skirt steak, approximately ½ lb per person for a generous portion. Apply salt sparingly. You can always add more later, but you can never take it off once added. Season two hours before cooking with a pinch of pepper, mustard powder and garlic salt.

Place meat on the hot barbecue grill.

Cooking Instructions

Place cuts of meat on a hot grill, leaving a narrow space between cuts for heat to pass through to ensure simultaneous "lateral" cooking. Ask guests how they want their meat cooked—rare, medium or well done. You can use a meat thermometer to ensure meat is cooked to an appropriate internal temperature.

If meat has bones, place bone towards the flame and turn over only when the heat has reached through the top of the meat facing away from the fire. If no bones, turn the meat over only when heat has reached the top of the cut.

Coordinate to serve meat simultaneously with side dishes. A good barbecue must be served sizzling hot. Sizzling is the meat's music. Don't miss it!

If you are cooking skirt steak, once cooked, cut against the grain into thin strips for easier serving. Enjoy it!

Argentines prefer to eat their barbecued meat with very few condiments, except chimichurri which is a typical Argentine sauce. It is very easy to prepare and adds a nice garlicky flavor to the meat. Ed enjoys fixing it himself!

The tradition continues with our Texan son-in-law, Karl!

Serves: 4-6

Chimichurri

Ingredients

6 cloves garlic, finely chopped

2 cups fresh Italian parsley chopped

1 tbsp kosher or pink salt

1 tsp crushed red pepper flakes

1 cup extra virgin olive oil

½ cup red wine vinegar

A touch of pepper and a pinch of mustard powder

Preparation

Mix the garlic, parsley, salt, pepper, mustard and red pepper flakes. Add the olive oil and vinegar and stir. Expose it to sunlight for two hrs until it sets.

Transfer to a serving bowl and spread it over barbecued meat, particularly beef. You can store any leftover in the refrigerator for future use.

Karina's Tribute

I am so happy my Mom's longtime dream of writing a cookbook has become a reality. This book encapsulates the family themes when I was growing up which I now carry on with my husband, Gary, and our children Vanessa, Sophia, Isabella and Nathan.

Having lived out of state for a few years, I also learned the themes in this book are applicable not only to our biological family, but the family of Christ as well. Not everyone has the blessing of living close to their blood relatives, but certainly we can all put into practice having fun, sharing good food, praying together, and ministering to those friends who become our family in Christ.

I would like to share **Ten Lessons** my Mom modeled with her life that Gary and I carry on with our family.

The first three life lessons are things my mom discouraged us from participating in because they are not honoring to God. They eat away at the fabric of relationships and rob us of joy, peace and freedom...

Don't Gossip

The Bible has several verses about gossip, but one my Mom quoted often was Proverbs 26:20, "Without wood a fire goes out; without a gossip a quarrel dies down" (NIV). Growing up, the image of a fire dying out without more fuel was a good way to see the damage gossip causes.

Don't Criticize Church Leaders

If visitors began to criticize their pastor or their church, my Mom would say, "Let's pray for them." She would explain that we are all sinful people and it's only natural pastors or church leaders will make mistakes, but it's not our place to criticize them. Instead, we should pray for them and bless them.

No Sarcasm or Passive Aggressive Comments

Sarcasm and passive aggressive comments are something I don't remember ever happening in our family. Sometimes we were around people who were being sarcastic and we could see how hurtful it was. Proverbs 26:18-19 (NIV), "Like a maniac shooting flaming arrows of death is one who deceives their neighbor and says, 'I was only joking!'"

Both sarcasm and passive aggressive comments give the impression of humor, but beneath the surface they are dishonest. It's humor at the expense of someone else, and in the long run it erodes trust and respect.

The next three life lessons are things my Mom has always done that enrich those around her...

Regularly Share Faith Building Testimonies

Something my parents have done from my earliest memory is to share edifying testimonies, whether it was stories of missionaries, heroes of the faith, answers to prayer or something that happened in their day. Most often, these testimonies were shared around the dinner table as the main topic of conversation. This is something Gary and I still do with our children. With our daughter away at college, it's something we also share in our family group text. It's a way to continually build our faith and see all that God is doing in our lives.

Have a Lifestyle of Prayer

My Mom and Dad, along with both my grandmothers, truly live a lifestyle of prayer that is as essential to them as breathing. 1 Thessalonians 5:17 (NIV), "... pray without ceasing..." Prayer is an ongoing, never ceasing conversation with God throughout the day and night. It's something my sisters and I adopted at an early age and continue to this day. As a child, and then as a parent, there's such a comfort in knowing I can call my Mom night or day and ask for prayer and she faithfully prays.

Give Generously to Those Who are Less Fortunate

Proverbs 31:20 (NIV), "She opens her hand to the poor and reaches out her hands to the needy." The entire chapter of Proverbs 31 describes my Mom, and especially verse 20. She and my Dad have always shared with the less fortunate. They do so joyfully, gladly, and most importantly, generously.

The last four life lessons are part of what makes my Mom my Mom. They are ways that bring peace and joy to the family and build strong relationships...

Encourage Imagination & Creativity by Trying New Things

My Mom is always learning and growing. Whether it's learning French, trying to recreate a recipe from a great meal she had at a restaurant, getting her degree in Interior Design as a brand new grandmother, keeping up with the quickly changing technology world, or adapting recipes to her grandchildren's dietary needs. She's an example of having an inquisitive mind and never being too old to learn something new. One day, she took my daughter Vanessa as a toddler to the park. They met another toddler named Allison who had just moved to California from England. When Vanessa and my Mom got home, they spoke in a British accent and had a proper English tea time in honor of Allison.

Celebrate Tea Time and Other Traditions

Since my Mom has British heritage, teatime is something we enjoy doing regularly. My sisters and I do it with our children as well. Many family gatherings will include china teacups, finger food, and lovely conversation. My daughter Sophia has hosted several themed tea parties for her cousins. It's a tradition that encourages practicing good manners both for old and young alike. One of my son Nathan's favorite traditions is spending Super Bowl Sunday at my parents' house and enjoying all the fun finger foods and munchies. Sometimes they are specialty foods my parents brought back from their travels. We always plan to eat dinner during halftime. The most memorable meal to date was Arroz Con Pollo (recipe on page 73). Every New Year's Day, for more than a decade, my family has met up

Karina's Tribute (continued)

with my parents for lunch at their favorite restaurant in Carmel, CA. After lunch, we always go for a walk down main street, stop in our favorite coffee shop for dessert, before resuming our walk. My daughter Isabella loves the ice cream they serve at the coffee shop and that's always the highlight of the day for her. One tradition I started when my girls were young was to have a Fall Soup party at our favorite park. Each one of the sisters brings a homemade soup, and my Mom brings yummy French bread and coffee. We always take a picture by the same tree. It's fun to see from year to year how much the kids have grown.

Model of the "Perfect" Mother-in-Law

My Mom is such an example of how to be a considerate or "perfect" mother-in-law. My husband enjoys spending time with my Mom, which I know is not the case for many husbands. My Mom never gives unsolicited advice. When she is a guest in our home, she is always positive and complimentary. She always sees the best in people and situations, and she's thoughtful and considerate. She is never pushy or controlling. In a word, my Mom is respectful of her sons-in-law and their role in the family. I hope to follow her amazing example when it's my turn to be a mother-in-law.

Devotion & Service to God

My Mother has lived a life of devotion first to God, then to her husband and children, and serving the Lord in word and deed. Our family has had many hard and trying times. Through sickness and health, scarcity and abundance, my Mom has remained steadfast in her devotion to the Lord. There is a reassurance and a strength I have drawn from in the trials of my own adult life.

Below I have listed some of my favorite excerpts from 1 Thessalonians chapter 5 which reflect the themes in this book, as well as the life of my Mother:

[13]…live in peace with each other…[14]encourage the disheartened, help the weak, be patient with everyone. [15]Make sure that nobody pays back wrong for wrong, but always strive to do what is good for each other and for everyone else. [16]Rejoice always, [17]pray continually, [18]give thanks in all circumstances; for this is God's will for you in Christ Jesus. [19]Do not quench the Spirit…[20]Do not treat prophecies with contempt, [21]but test them all; hold on to what is good, [22]reject every kind of evil. [23]May God himself, the God of peace, sanctify you through and through.

My prayer for you, dear reader, is that you will be encouraged to keep your eyes on Jesus so that you may be a blessing while you have fun, share good food, pray, and in turn minister to those around you.

~ *Karina McCann*

TRAVEL STORIES
FRANCE

THE COTE D' AZUR

When we were ministering in Europe, some friends took us to Nice where we had the best Nicoise Salad in the world. It was so good we wanted to have it every day! The Nicoise Salad is a French salad composed of tuna, green beans, hardboiled eggs, tomatoes, onions, capers, potatoes, olives and fresh butter lettuce.

One of the most spectacular views nearby is "Eze." It is a medieval village with a fortified castle overlooking the Mediterranean Sea. From the top, you have a breathtaking view of the coast. We went prayer walking in this area that needs it so much.

GRASSE

We went to Grasse, the world perfume capital, with shops and old town 18 km from Cannes. Grasse has been a perfume town ever since the 17th century. We went through the most beautiful fields of lavender. I love lavender and it was also my mother's favorite! We always had it in our home gardens. It is such a beautiful color, as well as having a wonderful scent.

Two Grasse perfumeries are represented in Eze Village: Galimard and Fragonard, both with shops, as well as a factory you can visit. The rich fragrances steaming from a simmering pot and the aroma that they bring is an unforgettable memory.

FOOD & FUN IN FRANCE

I always say, "You can't have a bad meal in France." Of course, I'm partial because my grandma was French. She was from Dieppe, in Normandy. To us, eating in France is always a delight, even on the train. Once we were going from Paris to Normandy and they served us an incredible lunch with a white tablecloth and a silver tray with a coffee pot and china cups. That was surprising for a train ride through the countryside, more so because the meal was included in the price of the fare!

The French take cooking and eating very seriously. The produce is always fresh.

Some dishes on the menu may not be available on any certain day because the chef did not approve of what came from the farm, which shows the pride they take in their food.

A funny thing happened to us when we were ministering in Paris. We decided to go to a very nice restaurant because it was our wedding anniversary and Ed wanted to treat me. That night we had an amusing experience with the wine steward. He came to our table and when we told him that we were not having wine, he was visibly disgusted, stomped his foot and exclaimed, "Oh, Americains!" He never returned to our table but would turn his back every time he passed by. We started laughing, and I asked Ed, "What if I had ordered a Coca-Cola instead?" Ed said they would have thrown us out on the street as undesirables. It was a fun-filled wedding anniversary that we'll never forget!

The next day we went on the River Seine dinner cruise which we turned into a prayer expedition, blessing the buildings dotting its banks. When the boat passed by Notre Dame, we felt a strong leading to intercede for that iconic place. It was so powerful. We asked the Lord to be merciful to France and to visit that beautiful nation.

Ross and Lynne Whitehill took us to beautiful places like this during a holiday in the Alsace region of France and Luxembourg.

A VERY FUNNY BLUNDER

In between ministry assignments, we squeezed in a visit to Le Mont Saint-Michel, pictured above, which is an island off the coast in Normandy. This is where they filmed The Scarlet Pimpernel, a movie that our family likes very much. After walking all the way to the top, we were hungry and found a bistro inside a cavern. We were dressed casually, but the restaurant was quite elegant (only the French would do such a thing in a rather rustic place).

It was hot, so I removed my jacket as we sat down. Suddenly, I realized that I was wearing an "In-N-Out Burger" T-shirt in this very French place! I quickly put my jacket back on, but it was so hot that I looked ridiculous. We laughed all through the meal. No wonder the waiter was giving me disapproving looks. He didn't say it, but I imagine him mumbling under his breath, "Americain…" except that I am more French than American. Very funny!

Side Dishes

Potato Gratin

Risotto

Dairy Potato Bake

Turkey Stuffing

Tuna Stuffed Tomatoes

Baked Carrots

Serves: 6

Potato Gratin

Ingredients

1 large clove garlic, peeled and mashed

1 stick butter, softened

2 ¼ cups half & half

1 ¼ tsp salt

⅛ tsp ground black pepper

Pinch of grated nutmeg

Pinch of cayenne pepper

2 lbs potatoes, peeled and sliced ⅛" thick

1 cup grated Gruyere, Cheddar or Parmesan cheese

Preparation

Pre-heat oven to 350°. Place large clove of garlic on cutting board and smash it with the side of a large knife. The peel will come off easily and now take the smashed garlic clove and rub bottom and sides of a gratin dish or shallow baking dish (8x8).

Mince remaining garlic and set aside. Spread dish with half the butter. Bring half & half, salt, pepper, nutmeg, cayenne, potatoes and garlic to a boil in medium saucepan over medium heat, stirring occasionally with wooden spoon (liquid will just barely cover potatoes). Reduce heat and simmer until liquid thickens, about 2 min.

Pour potato mixture into prepared dish and shake dish to distribute evenly. Gently press down potatoes until submerged in liquid; dot with remaining butter. Bake until top is golden brown (basting once or twice during first 45 min). 10 min before potatoes are done, sprinkle cheese on top and let brown for remaining time.

Let rest for 5 min and serve.

Risotto (Authentic Italian Style)

Ingredients

5 oz Arborio rice

1 tbsp butter

2 tbsp olive oil

3 ½ cups clear chicken broth (see recipe under Leek & Potato Soup), or any broth you like

1 small glass dry white wine

½ cup finely chopped onion

Salt and pepper

Preparation

Melt butter and oil in pan and then sauté onions for about 3 min. Add rice, stirring on low heat until toasted, about 2 min. Add wine and turn heat to medium. Stir until wine has evaporated. Stir in half the broth until liquid is absorbed. Continue adding broth little by little, stirring as you add (rice should absorb liquid as it cooks), until you've added all the liquid.

Keep stirring while the broth is being absorbed as this is the key to a good risotto!

Optional: Add ⅓ cup Parmesan cheese, or cooked and chopped shrimp, asparagus, green peas, carrots, mushrooms, or any vegetable of your liking.

Dairy Potato Bake

Ingredients

1 2-lb bag frozen hash brown potatoes, thawed

½ cup butter, melted

1 tsp salt (can use less)

Dash of pepper

½ cup chopped onion

1 can cream of chicken soup

1 12-oz carton sour cream

2 cups grated Cheddar cheese

2 cups crushed corn flakes

¼ cup melted butter

Preparation

In large bowl, stir together the potatoes, ½ cup butter, salt, pepper, onion, soup, sour cream and cheese. Pour mixture into buttered 9x13 dish. Top with corn flakes and the ¼ cup butter drizzled over. Bake at 350° for 1 hr.

Optional: You can make your own cream of chicken soup by using a chicken stock recipe (see page 57) and blending all the ingredients (except the chicken) to make it creamy. Or if you prefer a lighter dish, simply use the chicken stock without blending.

Turkey Stuffing

Ingredients

2 boxes cornbread stuffing

2 bunches green onions

4 cloves garlic

¾ cup parsley, chopped

4 tbsp vinegar

¾ tbsp all spice seasoning

½ tsp cloves

¼ tsp Tabasco sauce

Salt to taste

4 eggs, beaten lightly

2 cups chicken broth

Preparation

Mix first nine ingredients together. Add eggs and chicken broth. Fry in 3 tbsp butter, half the stuffing mixture at a time, then stuff the turkey.

Serves: 4

Tuna Stuffed Tomatoes

A good side dish! Great for summer.

Ingredients

4 large tomatoes

2 cans (6 oz) tuna

⅓ cup mayonnaise

1 tbsp lemon juice

½ cup cooked rice

2 tsp finely chopped onion

½ tsp salt

½ tsp pepper

Preparation

Cut tomatoes in half. Scoop out pulp from tomatoes (you can save the pulp to use in sauce or in another meal). Drain tomatoes face down.

Combine remaining ingredients and mix. Then fill tomatoes and keep in refrigerator until ready to serve. Decorate the tops with mayonnaise and olives if you'd like.

Serves: 2-4

Baked Carrots

Ingredients

2 cups carrots, cut up in small pieces

1 cup mayonnaise

3 tbsp horseradish

½ cup bread crumbs

½ small onion, grated

Preparation

Mix all ingredients together, place in a baking dish and cook at 350° for 20 min.

HEALTHY ALTERNATIVE: Instead of mayonnaise, you can use vegenaise, **an egg-free mayonnaise that is very tasty.**

"A cheerful heart is good medicine."
Proverbs 17:22

Slice of Life:
The Family that <u>HAS FUN</u> Together
STAYS TOGETHER

You will never regret laughing and playing with your family, nor will they!

It is important to make time to play with and have fun with your family since kids like to hang around those who play with them and enjoy their company. Laughter is medicine to the soul and to the body, especially after a hard day. If you have fun with your children now, they will trust you with their problems later because laughing together builds bridges.

Birthday parties have been a great source of joy for our family.

We have hosted some really entertaining events over the years: lip sync competitions, Hawaiian-themed parties, and even a groovy '70s costume party. For one of the birthdays, we had a square dance. We all wore cowboy hats and boots and had a professional square dance "caller" to lead the festivities. It was a blast.

During another birthday, a "food fight" using chocolate candies broke out around the table with our girls and some of their friends. We were all laughing so hard as we dodged the projectiles! Our dog enjoyed all the extra food that hit the floor that night. The most memorable times as a family are when we allow ourselves to be spontaneous.

Some of our fun family activities are: playing volleyball at the park nearby on weekends, bike riding on the Nature Trail, go-cart racing downtown, flying kites, and pool parties.

When we were looking for a house, we prayed for one with a swimming pool and the Lord answered our prayer. We appreciate so much having a pool

Our version of *The Brady Bunch*.

during the hot days and a Jacuzzi on the cold ones. Some of our most enjoyable times happen "in the water."

Playing with the kids helps strengthen bonds that are essential for a family to grow closer.

It's my hope and prayer that you will be able to make the time and find creative ways to have fun with your loved ones because the family that plays together stays together. Who wants to walk away from fun?

Desserts

Norma's Famous Chocolate Chip Cookies

Fresh Lemon Bars

Apple Coffee Cake

Delicious Chocolate Pie

Flan "De Luxe"

Chocolate Cake in a Mug

Homemade Crêpes

Lemon Cake

Classic Peach Cobbler

Banana Nut Cake

Easy Cookies

Rice Pudding

Tiramisu

Norma's Famous Chocolate Chip Cookies

Kelly is an amazing young lady who lived with us for three years. She used to make these often!

Ingredients

1 cup white sugar

1 cup brown sugar

1 cup butter, melted

2 tbsp water

2 eggs

3 cups rolled oats

1 ½ cups flour

1 tsp baking soda

16 oz chocolate chips (semi-sweet or milk chocolate)

Preparation

Heat oven to 350°F. In a large bowl, mix both sugars and melted butter together until blended. Stir in water and eggs until light and fluffy. Stir in oats, flour, and baking soda; stir in chocolate chips. Drop dough by rounded tablespoonfuls onto ungreased cookie sheet, about 2 in apart. Bake 10 to 12 min or until golden brown. Cool slightly; remove from cookie sheet to wire rack.

Our son-in-law Benjy's mother, Norma, was so fun and always brought delicious desserts to our family gatherings. This is her famous recipe.

Fresh Lemon Bars (Kelly's Bars)

Ingredients

1 cup butter

½ cup powdered sugar

1 tsp vanilla

2 cups flour

4 eggs

2 cups sugar

Zest of one lemon

6 tbsp fresh lemon juice

¼ cup powdered sugar for topping

Preparation

Pre-heat oven to 350°. Generously grease a 9x13 pan. In mixing bowl, combine butter, ½ cup powdered sugar and vanilla and beat until fluffy. Gradually add flour, mixing until well combined. Spread evenly in pan and bake for 20 min.

While crust bakes, in a bowl combine eggs, sugar, lemon zest and lemon juice. Stir to blend (don't beat) and pour mixture over baked crust layer. Return to oven and bake until topping is set and lightly browned (18-20 min). Sift additional powdered sugar over warm bars to generously coat. Cut into bars. Remove when cool.

Serves: 8

Apple Coffee Cake

Ingredients

1 ½ cups sifted flour

2 ¼ tsp baking powder

½ cup sugar

½ tsp salt

½ tsp cinnamon

1 egg

½ cup milk (preferably 2% or whole)

¼ cup butter, melted

1 ½ cups chopped Granny Smith apples (2-3 apples)

CrumbTopping:

½ cup sugar

¼ cup flour

2 tbsp butter

½ tsp cinnamon

Preparation

Mix sifted flour with other dry ingredients and set aside. Beat egg, add milk and melted butter. Pour wet ingredients into the dry ingredients and then add the uncooked chopped apples and mix well.

Pour into a well greased 8-inch square pan. Mix together the crumb topping ingredients and sprinkle over the top of the batter.

Bake at 400° for 25-30 min or until a toothpick inserted comes out clean.

Serves: 8

Delicious Chocolate Pie

Ingredients

2 cups heavy cream (keep divided)

¾ cup dark, semisweet chocolate chips

1 ¼ cups salted pretzels, crushed

6 tbsp melted butter

¾ cup firmly packed dark brown sugar (divided)

½ cup cream cheese, softened

⅓ cup creamy peanut butter

Chocolate shavings for garnish

Preparation

Melt chocolate chips and 1 cup heavy cream until chocolate melts, on the stove or in the microwave for a few seconds. Stir and chill in the refrigerator for 2 hrs. In a 9-inch pie dish, combine pretzels with butter and ¼ cup brown sugar and press into dish. Cover and refrigerate for 30 min.

Blend cream cheese, peanut butter and ¼ cup brown sugar with mixer at medium speed. Beat 1 cup heavy cream and gradually add in remaining ¼ cup brown sugar until soft peaks form. Fold into cream cheese mixture and spoon into prepared pie crust. Cover and refrigerate 1 hr. Whip chocolate cream at medium speed with mixer until creamy. Spread over pie and top with chocolate shavings. Refrigerate for at least 3 hrs before serving.

A great recipe to make with your children and you don't have to bake or cook it. It is well worth the time it takes to make it.

Serves: 4-6

Flan "De Luxe"

Ingredients

4 cups milk or half & half

¾ cup sugar

⅛ tsp salt

1 tsp vanilla extract

6 large eggs, well beaten

Preparation

Mix milk, sugar and salt and boil vigorously for 10 min (be careful that it doesn't overflow).

Add mixture to the eggs a little at a time, beating for 3 min while mixture cools. Stir in vanilla. Set oven to 300°. Pour mixture into a mold that has "caramelo" in it (see below). Bake using **Baño Maria** (instructions follow) for 1 ½ hours or until knife inserted in flan comes out clean. Chill in refrigerator. Unmold onto a dish with a raised edge to keep the caramelo from dripping off the sides.

Caramelo:

Pour 4 tbsp white sugar in mold. Brown over burner until it melts, covering the bottom until it hardens.

Baño Maria:

Take a larger pan with some water in it and place the mold inside; place both in the oven. Make sure water doesn't get into the flan.

Optional:

In Argentina, they serve flan with a spoonful of cream and a spoonful of dulce de leche, a type of caramel sauce.

One of our grandsons is lactose intolerant, so I make his flan with almond milk.

Serves: 1

Chocolate Cake in a Mug

Ingredients

4 tbsp sugar

4 tbsp flour

2 tbsp cocoa

1 egg

3 tbsp whole milk

3 tbsp vegetable oil

3 tbsp chocolate chips (semi-sweet)

½ tsp vanilla extract

1 lg coffee mug (microwave safe)

Preparation

Put dry ingredients into the mug and mix well. Add the egg and mix well. Pour in milk and oil and mix again. Add chocolate chips and vanilla and mix again.

Place mug in the microwave and cook for 3 min. The cake will rise over the top. Use caution as the mug will be hot.

Allow to cool and enjoy.

Every time I go to our daughters' homes, the grandkids ask me, "Can you make us panqueques with dulce de leche?" It's as easy as making pancakes and you don't need a special pan. A small non-stick pan will do. Here is a simple step-by-step recipe.

Serves: 4-6

Homemade Crêpes

Ingredients

1 cup flour

⅛ tsp salt

2 eggs

1 cup milk

2 tbsp unsalted butter, melted

Preparation

Whisk everything together in a bowl until smooth. Batter will be runny. Heat a non-stick pan over medium high heat. Coat pan with melted butter or cooking spray. Using a ladle, pour a few tablespoons of crêpe batter in the center of the pan. When it's brown, turn it over and cook a few moments longer.

We fill them with "dulce de leche," then roll them up. Dulce de leche is a caramel type of jam common in Argentina and found in international markets.

You can use the crêpe batter for sweet or savory dishes!

Serves: 6
Lemon Cake

Ingredients

1 pkg lemon cake mix
4 eggs
1 pkg (small) lemon pudding mix
1 cup boiling water
1 tbsp lemon extract
¾ cup vegetable oil

Preparation

Combine pudding and boiling water until dissolved. Let cool. Mix all ingredients together for 4 min. Pour into a greased 9x13 pan, or two square or round pans. Bake at 350° for 25-35 min or until cake pulls away from sides of pan and top is set.

Remove from oven and prick with a fork all over the top. Spoon on glaze while hot so it seeps into the holes.

Glaze: Mix 1 cup powdered sugar and juice of ½ large lemon until smooth.

This is the first cake we ate when we came to study in the U.S.A. in 1970. I thought it was so easy using a box cake mix when we were used to making cakes from scratch in Argentina!

FUNNY & SAD

There was a place close to our house that served fresh food. We would go when we returned from a trip and had no food in the refrigerator. There was a dessert that was our favorite: Auntie Aldo's Bread Pudding. It was bread based and had raisins, apples, a swirl of caramel sauce, and was served hot a la mode with a scoop of ice cream. Yummy!

One day, I said to Aldo (the owner), "Your auntie must have been a wonderful cook," and he started laughing.

"My aunt didn't know how to cook," he replied, "not even a hardboiled egg."

"Why did you name the dessert after her?" I asked.

"Oh, because it was her favorite dessert."

The sad part of the story is that the restaurant closed down suddenly. Our grandson Maxi called us one day while we were traveling overseas to give us the bad news. He was almost in tears because we used to take him there for the best pizza in town, and we had many gatherings there with family and friends. We miss you, Megabytes.

Serves: 4-6

Classic Peach Cobbler

Ingredients

4 cups frozen peach slices
1 cup melted butter

Crumble topping:
2 cups uncooked, plain Quaker oats
1 box white cake mix
2 cups brown sugar
2 tsp ground cinnamon
2 tsp ground cloves
1 tsp ground allspice
½ tsp salt
2 cups butter

Preparation

In a 9x13 baking dish, place the frozen peaches and drizzle melted butter. In a large bowl, mix all the dry ingredients, then break in the butter until very fine pieces scattered throughout. Put topping on top of the peach/butter preparation in the baking dish. Place in a pre-heated 350° oven for 45 min or until bubbly and browning on top.

Note: You can replace the peaches with frozen blackberries or raspberries, etc.

Great with ice cream!

Serves: 4-6

Banana Nut Cake

Ingredients

⅔ cup butter
2 ½ cups sifted cake flour
1 ⅔ cups sugar
1 tsp baking soda
1 ¼ tsp baking powder
1 tsp salt
1 ¼ cups fully ripe bananas, mashed
⅔ cup buttermilk
2 eggs
⅔ cup chopped walnuts

Preparation

Beat softened butter. Sift in dry ingredients. Add bananas and half the buttermilk. Mix until all flour is incorporated. Beat on high speed for 2 min. Add remaining buttermilk and eggs; beat 2 min more. Fold in nuts. Bake in two parchment lined 9x1½ round pans at 350° for about 35 min. Cool 10 min in pans. Remove and let cool completely. Spread first layer with ⅓ of cocoa whipped cream and top with 2 sliced bananas. Add second layer and frost top and sides with remainder.

Cocoa Whipped Cream: Combine ½ cup sugar, ⅓ cup cocoa and 1 ½ cups heavy cream. Chill at least one hour. Beat until stiff.

Easy Cookies

Ingredients

1 cup peanut butter
1 egg
1 cup sugar

Preparation

Combine ingredients and form into balls.
Flatten balls with a fork and place on a cookie
sheet. Bake at 335° for 8 min.

Very fun and easy to make with the little
ones! Even a four year-old can make these!

Rice Pudding

Ingredients

4 cups milk
½ cup sugar
½ cup rice
1 tsp vanilla extract
Rind of one orange
Optional: 1 tsp nutmeg

Preparation

In a saucepan, bring ingredients to a boil,
then lower heat. Cook for 25 min or until desired consistency. My husband likes it thick;
my grandkids like it watery. Cool and enjoy.
In Argentina, we eat it with a spoonful of
dulce de leche, a type of caramel sauce. Some
grocery stores carry it, or you can find it at
international markets.

Serves: 6

Tiramisu

Ingredients

24 Ladyfinger Italian Cookies

Coffee/Rum Filling:
1 cup strong coffee, brewed
½ cup rum
¼ cup white granulated sugar
Combine ingredients over stovetop on low heat until sugar dissolves into the liquid and then set aside to cool.

Mascarpone Cream Filling:
16 oz store bought mascarpone cream hand whipped with ½ cup powdered sugar until incorporated
OR
Make your own mascarpone substitute by blending with an electric blender 1 cup cream cheese with 4 tbsp sour cream plus ½ cup powdered sugar. Then whip 8 oz heavy whipping cream until stiff peaks form and gently fold into the cream cheese mixture by hand until incorporated.

Topping:
1 cup heavy whipping cream
½ cup white granulated sugar
Beat together the whipping cream and sugar until stiff peaks form.

¼ cup grated or shaved dark chocolate

Preparation

Begin by placing one layer of Ladyfingers at the bottom of a 4x8 loaf pan. Drizzle this layer with the prepared Coffee/Rum filling. Slather about ⅓ inch of the Mascarpone Cream filling onto this first layer.

Repeat layering process until all ingredients are used up. Top the entire thing with whipped cream topping, cover with plastic wrap and refrigerate for at least 2 hrs or overnight. When ready to serve, garnish with chocolate shavings and cut into slices.

TRAVEL STORIES
AUSTRIA, SWITZERLAND, GERMANY

AUSTRIA

There are so many beautiful places in the world. Salzburg, Austria, is one of them, with its rolling hills, rich culture and Baroque architecture. Standing beside the Salzach River, you see domes, cliff top fortresses and the mountains, a formidable and incredible view. Salzburg was the home of Mozart. The scenery, the skyline, the music and history of Salzburg delight your senses.

You can almost hear Julie Andrews singing The Sound of Music while you walk its narrow streets.

When we went for the first time, we thought that someday it would be nice to bring our grandchildren to do the tour of the filming of the Sound of Music movie. It's a wonderful tour of a wonderful movie. Well, the Lord granted us that blessing!

Marilyn and Ken and their three girls were able to come. They enjoyed it so much that they sang the songs the whole time.

One night, we went to dinner at a monastery turned restaurant up on a hill.

Their youngest daughter was only three at the time and was very tired. While we were waiting for the food (it takes much longer to be served than in the U.S.), Marilyn bought a big pretzel for her, and as soon as she set it on the table, she fell fast asleep using the pretzel as a pillow. Ken had to carry her all the way down the mountain, at night, back to the hotel.

SWITZERLAND

The best fondue we ever had was in Switzerland, of course, and the most memorable one in Gruyere, a picture-perfect medieval town on a small hill with a castle. At the foot of the Pre-Alps, Gruyere's architecture is quite charming. The town has given its name to the region and to its world famous cheese.

I bought cowbells there for our grandchildren, and they still have them. God created beautiful landscapes around the world for us to enjoy. Make sure you take time today to enjoy the sights all around you.

GERMANY

I have another story about Ken and Marilyn's youngest daughter. We were in Munich and she was craving sausages, so our host went to get her one. "We have the best sausages right here in Munich. They are very special and world famous," he said. He returned with a Weisswurst, a white sausage.

Our granddaughter looked at the white sausage and although she didn't want to say anything, it wasn't the sausage she was hoping for. So, Ken went running down the street and brought back a hot dog for her which she easily recognized and ate happily.

Munich Weisswurst is a Bavarian specialty made from the finest cuts of meat with mild spices and it's often served with pretzels and special sweet mustard. All three sisters have never forgotten Munchen, the Alps and the white Weisswurst!

Beverages

El Mate

Russian Tea

Non-alcoholic Sangria

New Season Smoothie

A Green Drink

El Mate

Mate ("mah-tay") is a traditional drink in Argentina where it is considered the "national infusion." It is prepared by steeping dried leaves of "yerba mate" in hot water and is sipped using a metal straw from a hollow calabash gourd. The straw is called a *bombilla* in Spanish.

Modern, commercial straws are usually made of nickel silver (called alpaca), stainless steel, or hollow cane. The gourd is known as mate and the hot water is supplied from a thermos. You can drink mate sweetened with sugar or "amargo" (bitter).

The preparation consists of filling the gourd with yerba, pouring hot (but never boiling) water over the leaves, and drinking through the bombilla which acts as a filter so as to draw only the liquid and not the yerba leaves.

In the province where I grew up, they add an herb called peperina (peppermint) for flavor.

Mate is traditionally enjoyed in close, social settings such as family gatherings or with friends. The drink has a strong cultural significance, both in terms of national identity, as well as socially.

In Northern Argentina they sometimes drink it cold in a hollow grapefruit because of the hot and semi-tropical weather there. The locals call it *terere*, a word in the Guarani dialect.

Our own mate gourd has accompanied us to all the countries where we have traveled! Although Ed doesn't drink mate, he likes to serve it to me.

Makes: 2 quarts

Russian Tea

Ingredients

5 regular black tea bags

5-6 cups boiling water

½ cup sugar

1 tsp lemon or orange peel

12 allspice, crushed

1 whole cinnamon stick

1-2 tbsp whole cloves

¼ cup lemon juice

1 can frozen orange juice (6 oz)

2 cups pineapple juice

Preparation

Combine the first seven ingredients in large bowl and let steep at least 45 min. Strain spiced tea into a half gallon container and add the fruit juices. Reserve cinnamon stick and place in final tea mixture. Refrigerate. Warm before serving.

Makes: 2 quarts

Non-alcoholic Sangria

Ingredients

2 cups black tea (brewed and chilled)

1 cinnamon stick

½ cup sugar

3 cups pomegranate juice

1 cup freshly squeezed orange juice

1 medium orange sliced into thin rounds

1 medium lemon sliced into thin rounds

Optional: 1 medium lime sliced into thin rounds

1 apple, cored and cut into ½" chunks

3 cups carbonated water

Preparation

Combine all ingredients (except carbonated water) one hour in advance or chill overnight. Just before serving, stir in carbonated water and serve over ice.

Serves: 2-4

New Season Smoothie

Ingredients

2 celery stalks

2 carrots

½ beet

½ apple

Bunch of spinach

2 leaves kale

Small piece of ginger root

Small handful of sunflower seeds

1 spoon of Hemp protein powder

Preparation

Blend everything until liquid and enjoy a healthy drink.

Serves: 1-2

A Green Drink

Ingredients

1 cucumber, peeled & chopped

2 handfuls chopped kale

2 celery stalks, chopped

1 lemon, juiced

2 green apples

Preparation

Blend well.

Celebrations & Holidays

When you gather around the table, go beyond simply saying grace and add praise and worship to it, and while eating the food, do it joyfully since God has given everything for us to enjoy. And don't forget to praise the hands that prepared it.

One of the traditions that Ed instituted was that when the food was set on the table, he and the girls (and guests if they were present) would shout: "Viva la Cocinera!" and clap. This means, "Three cheers for the Cook!" in Spanish. I always enjoyed that.

For Easter, we usually prepare a tea party in the backyard so we can enjoy the beautiful spring weather. We read Scriptures and sing "He Lives," one of our favorite songs/hymns.

On Memorial Day and the 4th of July, the menu includes "Choripanes," a typical barbecued Argentine sausage served on French bread eaten as a sandwich. Then Ed places the wonderful cuts of beef on the grill and the ladies prepare a variety of salads and side dishes to accompany the meat.

In Argentina, barbecuing is a male thing. Men are very protective of that turf and they take pride in serving the "Asado," as it is called, sizzling.

For Thanksgiving, Christmas and New Year's, our celebrations are indoors since it's Winter in the Northern Hemisphere, but they remain centered around homemade food, fun, and expressions of our faith through song, prayer and testimonies.

On Thanksgiving, Ed always reads an inspirational story about the pilgrims with the kids sometimes dressed up in typical costumes. It's great to hear everyone share what

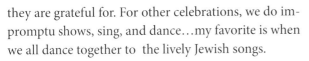

they are grateful for. For other celebrations, we do impromptu shows, sing, and dance…my favorite is when we all dance together to the lively Jewish songs.

Eating is a good way to keep up with traditions. Our children love traditions!

Psalm 34:8 says, "O taste and see that the Lord is good." God's recipe for happiness is guaranteed. The Psalmist urges us to try the Lord (like you would try a tasty dish), and see for yourself. We should also be more than eager to "taste" the Lord.

Marilyn wrote this in a cookbook she gave me for my birthday one year:

Dearest Mommy,
You taught me to enjoy cooking delicious food for my husband, family and friends (like you!). I love you and praise the Lord for giving me the best mami in the world (I want to be more like you).
Love,
Marilyn

A Godly Family Legacy

MY PARENTS

My mother Matilde's ancestry is British and French, so she could make a delicious High Tea, but also French Onion Soup. Besides cooking, she also enjoyed reading and sometimes I found her in the kitchen stirring a French béchamel sauce and reading a book at the same time! For our birthdays she always gave us books about heroes of the faith.

But the best legacy was her love for the Lord, her commitment to serve Him, and prayer. She was an inspiration and everybody loved her. She helped the poor and the rich alike. My father, Luis Palau, Sr., was a businessman who, after receiving the Lord, planted many churches in Argentina before he died at a young age. I thank the Lord for a righteous family heritage.

My siblings (left to right): Martha, Ketty, Luis, Margarita, Jorge and me. My sister Matil is pictured in the inset since it's next to impossible to capture the seven of us all together!

I am so happy that they all serve the Lord and, above everything else, they love to tell people about Jesus, just like my parents did and taught us to do!

ED'S PARENTS

Ed's mother, Maria Teresa, being Italian, makes the best homemade pasta in the world. She is also an inspiration to everyone who knows her. She has strong faith in the Lord and a powerful gift of service; helping others is her joy.

Even today, at 93, she is thinking of others and blessing them all the time. She made my wedding gown and, given the chance, would have been a great designer, a nurse, or a chef. Her specialty? Spinach Ravioli with Bolognese Sauce.

Her husband Omar, Ed's dad (now with the Lord), was a corporate executive and vocational politician. He was an atheist who enjoyed debating about religion until he met Jesus! And like the Apostle Paul, he became an apologist for the Gospel. He planted a church that today is one of the largest in the region.

Ed's only sibling, Maria Rosa, inherited Teresa's gifts for cooking and hospitality. She and her husband Ricardo, along with their five children, their spouses and grandchildren, also serve the Lord faithfully.

I praise the Lord for my loving in-laws and for their spiritual heritage.

Love Part 2: From Ruth to Ed

and the two shall become one...

My beloved Eddie:

From the moment I met you, I knew that we were made for each other. The Lord brought us together for a marriage made in heaven. You are an example in every way. There are no words to fully describe all that you are because you are truly exceptional.

Your affection is so sweet. I could not live without it. I love every minute I share with you; I can never get enough. You are fun to be with. You are the best husband, a great father and grandfather. The more I know you, the more I admire you.

There is no perfect husband, but you certainly come very close to it! I love serving the Lord together with you and with our children and grandchildren. On our wedding bands we inscribed: "In God we will do mighty works" (Ps. 108:13). We have seen this promise fulfilled indeed!

I have not met another servant of God like you, so humble and still effective; hardworking but always making time for others; busy but not hectic; anointed but not boastful. You are a true example of a servant-leader. You live what you preach. I am so proud of you and I know the Lord is, too.

Your companionship and friendship are priceless. Just the thought of you gives me instant joy and safety. How much more your company!

Today, I love you more than yesterday, but less than I will love you tomorrow. What an exciting prospect.

Yours yesterday, today and forever.

Ruthie

Ed's Tribute to Ruth:
You are My Eternal Sunshine

After eloquently describing a Worthy Woman, Proverbs 31 states, "Her children rise up and bless her; Her husband, also, and he praises her by saying, 'Many women have done nobly but you excel them all.'"

Our four daughters have done so already, and now it is my turn to praise Ruth. It is patently obvious that she is beautiful, intelligent, articulate, elegant and spiritual. All of that is there for anyone to see. But she has another remarkable virtue that is not so obviously on display: an extraordinary inner strength that comes from a perfect combination of a tender heart and a soul made of titanium as it befits someone who is so splendidly regal. As a result, her grace under fire is stunning. Let me tell you about some "private stories behind the public person."

After studying in the USA, we returned to Argentina to launch our ministry at the height of the Dirty War, a national tragedy that took 30,000 innocent lives. The first day we moved into a house, a fierce machine gun battle erupted on our sidewalk. When I threw myself over our girls while bullets flew, Ruth was right there next to me, like a mother hen protecting her baby chicks at the risk of her own life.

Some time later, when she was held by robbers at gunpoint on the floor of a pharmacy, she had the presence of mind to surreptitiously take off her wedding ring and hide it so that something so precious to both of us would not be stolen. When our car was pinned down in a battle between police and guerrillas, she never panicked. When I received death threats from the right and from the left for preaching the Gospel and refusing to take sides, not once did she say, "Let's pack up and go." The night a posse waited in front of our house to take me while I was ministering in another town, with no phone available to call for help, she prayed for a miracle...and my car broke down preventing me from returning until they had left.

She survived leukemia and meningitis, and while I sat by her bed, holding her hand and praying, she constantly radiated strength to our girls and me. Like Gibraltar, she will never sink, but unlike the Rock, she can soar like an eagle with wings of faith. My heart is fully entrusted to her. The last thing I do at night is reach for her hand and place it on my heart to hear her pray for me. And before dawn breaks, I reach for that hand again for her to pray as the day begins. She is my best friend, my confidant, my counselor, my personal intercessor and the love of my life.

How central she is to who I am became painfully evident when she underwent a risky medical procedure that instead of three hours went on for almost eight due to complications. In the waiting room, I was a tower of strength—fielding reports, mobilizing prayer, and reassuring everybody. She came out well, but later that night, when I found myself "sleeping single in a double bed" because she had to stay at the hospital, it hit me like a ton of bricks that she could have died that morning.

I looked to her side of the bed which faces East, to the spot on her pillow where every morning I wait for the light of dawn to explode in a sea of gold when it hits her blond hair, and I was devastated by the thought that I could have lost her. That prospect was so overwhelming that I cried out to God, "It would be as if the sun were to never come up again, leaving me in perpetual darkness. Lord, help me, please! I cannot conceive life without her!" And God went on to say, "When someone you love so much comes to Heaven, you must look for the sun to rise on the West instead of on the East, because it will rise, for sure, but from a different direction."

After pondering the divine metaphor for a while, I finally understood that the sweet moments we enjoy daily are the projection of what is already in our hearts. The sun is the heart radiating and the moon in our mind reflecting it. At that moment, it dawned on me how important the memories that we build together are because *memory is something that death can never kill.*

Today, it is my privilege to praise her for everything that is so obvious to everybody, but also for that extraordinary inner strength that I get to admire up close that has made me the man I am today and encourages me to become a better one tomorrow.

Yes, my dearest Ruthie, I rise up, along with our daughters, sons-in-law, grandchildren and spiritual children on every continent on earth, and I praise you as the most virtuous woman I know!

You are my sunshine indeed!

Yours forever,

Ed

The smiling faces of loved ones are bright stars that illuminate our path through the twilight of life...

...The path of the righteous is like the light of dawn that shines brighter and brighter until the full day.

PROVERBS 4:18

The Most Important Truth...

Every good thing you have seen in this book is the result of God's love. We are clay and He is the Potter who molds us and repairs us when we are broken because He is such a loving God. I give Him all the glory, honor and praise.

In closing, I wish to share what is to me the most important truth:

God loves people and families and He wants the very best for all of us. But the devil came to steal, to kill and to destroy in order to separate us from God. This is why God sent Jesus to rescue us (John 10:10).

"For God so loved the world that He gave His one and only Son, that whoever believes in Him shall not perish but have eternal life."
(John 3:16)

Whatever the devil has done to you, Jesus wants to undo it because He came to destroy the works of the evil one (see I John 3:8).

Jesus says, "Behold, I stand at the door and knock. If anyone hears my voice and opens the door, I will come in" (Revelation 3:20). The day I invited Him to come into my heart, my life changed forever. So did Ed's life when he did the same. We have seen our daughters experience this, as well. Jesus is the source of every good thing that I have been able to share in this book. If you have not done it yet, or if you have walked away from Him, I encourage you to invite Jesus to come into your life by praying this prayer:

Lord Jesus, thank you for what you did for me on the Cross. I now confess my need for forgiveness and I receive you as my Lord and Savior. Amen.

"To all who receive Him, He gave the right to become children of God."
(John 1:12)

If you did this, you have become a child of God.

Welcome to the Family of God!

~ Ruth Palau Silvoso

Acknowledgments

First and foremost, I want to praise the Lord for His faithfulness, grace, and love. I praise you, God, for your bountiful provision and blessings.

I want to thank my wonderful husband, Ed, for always affirming my food, thanking me for my cooking, and giving me ideas of what to cook when I've needed inspiration. You are my best friend, and I love you dearly.

Our daughter, Jesica, for encouraging and inspiring me to write this book. Thank you for all your help.

Our beloved executive assistant, Cindy Oliveira, for transcribing and helping organize the material, and her dear son, Isaac, who contributed his photographic talent, too. They are such a blessing!

Our precious friend, Danielle Guzman, for all the professional photography. She is a treasure indeed!

The graphic designer, Andrew Isaacs of i6 Graphics, for his God-given creativity.

My wonderful children, grandchildren and family, for always blessing me with so much joy. I am so thankful for you and I love you with all my heart.

To God be the glory forever and ever!

P.S. Pets are family, too!

Contact the Author

Ruth Palau Silvoso

TRANSFORM OUR WORLD
P.O. Box 20310
San Jose, CA 95160-0310

Email: ruthsilvoso@transformourworld.org

Visit our website for inspiring resources and events:
www.transformourworld.org